INNES UNPLUGGED

Innes unplugged

Allan F Brack

Cast of Characters

Duncan Innes - Independent Investigator/fixer for the Federal reserve

Alan MacDonald - Federal Reserve Security IT Head

Casey O'Brien - D.C. Detective former girlfriend of Innes

George Allyson - V.P. of the USA

Haughton - Federal Reserve Banker

Nigel Levick - Bank of England

Jessica Sierakowski - Lawyer, girlfriend of Innes

Helen Matsumoto - Assassin

Lt. Fischer - D.C. detective

Otto Sternberg - European Central Banker Frankfurt

Christian Allyson - V.P. son and head of Alltel

Mr. Assisi - Kuwaiti Banker

Erich Kochan - Christian Allyson assistant

Hans Ritter - Christian Allyson assistant

Marlee - S.African Lady Friend of Innes

ONE BANKER DOWN

The only noticeable faults in the painting were two small, bullet holes, of just a few millimeters in diameter, at the right bottom corner of the painting; below the feet of the flower seller. A casual glance would miss it altogether. Of the three fired, the second was two centimeters higher; a perfect hit, in the center of a sunflower, making it all but invisible. The third shot was evident between the victim's eyes lying below the painting. The shot was equidistance from each eye: centered, round, and bloodless; making the other two in the wall painting mute. The man was dead. His body was sprawled on the floor in a very unnatural position. Pants around the ankles, shirt halfway up his torso, arms spread out as if on a cross. The facial expression was that of pure surprise. The large window facing the garden was ajar, with curtains billowing in the draft. The sound would carry but dampened on such a night. With snow outside gently falling and all else still, the neighbors would have heard the shots as muffled pops. Snow always acts as a sound dampener. The room was cold. The victim didn't care.

He wrote in his notebook to have the patrolman have a word with anyone within earshot. The detective walked over to the picture window and looked out over the patio. Just below the doorframe, footsteps were visible as indentations leading away from the house. They were filling rapidly with fresh snow. He used his cell phone to take pictures before the tracks were completely covered by snow. The killer must have entered the home from another avenue, choosing to leave via the patio. In the far corner of the room was a small dog bowl filled with water; however, no dog. Looking back at the patio it was obvious the dog had gone out earlier. The tracks had already begun to disappear entirely; while the killer's footsteps seemed fresher and deeper. From the size of the prints, the killer could not have been very big; maybe a woman?

A siren could be heard in the distance coming closer with each new wail. He looked up at the patrol officer in the doorway and nodded towards the main entrance. The officer did not need another invitation. He hurried off to answer the as-yet-unheard doorbell.

"Are you sure he lives alone?"

The remaining patrolman answered in the affirmative. He had been through the entire house and other than the Homicide Lieutenant no one else was visibly there. The upstairs bedrooms were empty and gave the appearance of being unused. The kitchen seemed pristine and unused. One car in the garage with no traces of snow or water on the floor confirmed it had been there for at least two days. The snow had been falling off and on since Sunday.

"Check out the neighbors. See if anyone heard the shots or found the dog."

She sat behind the wheel of her car two blocks from the home she had recently left. A patrol car drove past her, pulling into the driveway of the home, behind the other officer's cruiser. It's flashing blue lights contrasting with the snow and reflected off the myriad of flakes falling on her car. The blue gave the area an aura of eeriness. Her window was slightly cracked, allowing cold air to circulate, creating a cloud on each exhale. The air itself was crisp. She squinted slightly to see the people moving about behind the large picture window. One uniformed officer was staring downwards at another person kneeling before what must be the body. The kill had been simple. Convince the mark that she was there to pleasure him; and when at his most vulnerable point of dropping his pants, pull the trigger. She had fired three times. Normally it would have taken only one shot, but this mark panicked on seeing the emerging gun and jumped backwards, an unusual move. Most would have dodged left or right; rarely backward. But it didn't matter in the end. His pants had tangled his legs, leaving him prone on the floor for her to step forward and neatly place her third shot. Another siren could be heard fast approaching; an ambulance arriving a little late to matter. The Medical Examiner would follow shortly. Rolling her window up, she started the engine and pulled out of the parking space, before the ambulance would arrive. Slowly she drove past the house, now illuminated by patrol car lights, and headed toward the airport. Her flight to Miami was at 10 p.m. More than enough time for dinner; even considering the rental return and a phone call. This job had indeed been a simple one. Her fee would be deposited in Switzerland, her employer pleased, and two weeks off were something to look forward to, in the sun; no snow!

The headline read 'Government official of the Federal Reserve DC, found murdered in the home'. 'Homicide detectives were unavailable for comment, however, the Chief of Police in Washington, D.C. noted 'he was confident that this was a robbery, although nothing appeared missing as yet'. Papers, in today's world, did not always make sense. Duncan knew the article certainly didn't; still, it held his attention. Why would anyone want to kill a Federal Reserve executive? To what end? As he thought about motive or lack thereof, his cell phone rang.

"Yes."

"Hi, Duncan. I take it you have been following the news about our banker friend?"

Alan McDonald was asking the question. Alan had been using Duncan Innes as an outside consultant for a decade; a title that might be considered a misnomer, considering the line of work Innes practiced. Consultants rarely fired Glocks even when provoked.

"Doesn't make a lot of sense to me, Alan."

He poured another cup of coffee.

"Well Duncan, it never does. What I need to know is who and why. Of course, what we do about it is the follow on."

"I'll get on it, but the police footprint might be a little large at the moment."

Duncan looked over at the muted TV screen running updates on the murder. This would make the whole process difficult.

"Duncan, I don't care. Find out: who, why, and get back to me."

The phone clicked off. He put his now empty coffee cup in the sink, ran some hot water over it, and then moved to the bedroom. A quick shower and the day would begin. Duncan had won the Ironman competition two years in a row ten years earlier. His six-foot-four frame remained lean; a testament to a vigorous training regime adhered to with almost maniacal dedication. Slight touches of grey peppered his dark hair; otherwise no visible signs of aging. Good genes were the accepted general consensus. He had run five miles that morning prior to his primary client's phone call and planned on a few hours at the gym. The job was always feast or famine. His apartment in D.C. was only two blocks from the workout center; which allowed guests in at all hours of the day and night. Yuppie heaven for the 5 a.m. set. Back in the bedroom, Duncan dressed in black slacks, light blue pinstriped shirt, Nicole Miller tie and blue blazer. The 9 mm Glock finished off his sartorial endeavors, leaving only the alarm system to be activated as he headed out the door for his first meeting of the day. Prior to showering, Duncan had emailed a detective on the D.C.P.D. and asked for a quick meet. They had been friends for the past five years, intimate friends for the previous five. Neither could answer why the relationship had shifted from lovers to friends, and neither would have cared to speculate. It just was!

Traffic was light; even D.C. respected snow. What made the drive difficult was driver experience. DC is not, nor ever was, filled with people that could actually drive; let alone in heavy weather. The flakes still fell; but had slowed. There was hope. He passed an accident on Dupont Circle, but otherwise, the ride in was uneventful. Casey O'Brien would already have arrived at the Deli and certainly would be frowning on why she was always first to arrive. Her annoyed state was confirmed as Duncan entered the Deli cum Bakery and sat down across from her.

"I thought I might hear from you this morning. Boss getting nervous about the loss of a government employee?"

"Certainly interested; how are you?"

She laughed. They both put their orders in for coffee and bagels, Duncan's second breakfast of the day.

"I am fine and really happy this is not my case."

She still looked very good peering over the coffee cup.

"Why, we could have worked together."

He smiled as he said it, knowing the reaction.

"You never work 'together' with anyone. Besides, the higher-ups want this handled discretely and with as little noise as possible." She couldn't help but notice the intent look from the female barista towards Duncan. Some things never change.

Duncan watched her attack the bagel with occasional sips of coffee. There was something feral about the way she devoured her food. That had always held a fascination since he first met Casey. Her excuse was 'cops on duty had to eat and run'. No time for dainty bites and sips from a demitasse. A small crumb hung from her lower lip as she started in again for another bagel ambush. Duncan admired her tenacity and of course, raw good looks. She had: dirty blonde hair, usually in a ponytail for work, gold-green eyes, that could flash with anger when provoked, and a mellow aura surrounded her when she was at ease. The latter attribute made her the perfect interrogator. Perps, more often than not, forgot who was asking the questions; giving up far more than they intended to at any given sitting.

"Any news at the station?"

"Too early" Casey replied.

"Okay, but do me a favor, let me know if you hear anything?"

Casey paused chewing and looked at Duncan expectantly. Since when had she not been doing favors? Some nerve to suggest this might be the first turn down, she thought.

"I will call you if something turns up, but I doubt this will be a simple one. This one smells bad."

"Don't they all?" as he finished the last bit of bagel.

Chapter 2

Miami

She preferred the hotel pool rather than the beach. For her, pool service concerns came before: sunburns, warm ocean water, and flotsam from passing ships. It was late afternoon and slowly boredom was creeping into her daily routine. One week in the sun was great; two bordered on being roasted medium rare with appointments made in dermatology offices to repair the damage. The feelings of snow had been warmed away by the sun. Most of the other guests at the pool looked at one another with guilt for being here rather than working in the drudgery of the north. Her laptop perched on her tanned legs. To her right was a small table, at lounge chair height, supporting a gin and tonic with the obligatory lime overseeing the ice. Beads of condensation ran the length of the half-empty glass. A coaster ensured the absorption of moisture, preventing the sudden shock of cold droplets falling on her, when she sipped. The pool was practically empty for this time of year. Snowbirds typically dominated the landscape between November and April. A few children played some indescribable game at the shallow end, as parents looked on with a sense of quasi-concern. A waiter leaned against the Tiki-Bar talking with a young bartender dressed in a loincloth and petite bra.

She had been lounging here for a week; which felt like a month. While the trip up north to D.C. had been very profitable, it was just too easy. An older man with the suspicions of a puppy offered no real challenges. Perhaps it was better this way. No challenge, large reward. It seemed appropriate in light of her professional choices. She pushed her hair back from her forehead and thought of where she might have dinner that evening. Shooters in Lauderdale seem like a good idea. Lots of people, lots of noise; very few questions; drunks easily passed off to easier marks. She knew if she wanted physical companionship, it would do as a simple trolling point.

It was time to baste her other side, think about leaving to change and go out. She flipped over, put her head down on the towel, rolled onto a pillow, and enjoyed watching the scene unfold of the waiter hitting on the bartender. It was the bell tone from her computer that re-focused her attention. Incoming mail from the U.K. only meant a new job. Boredom would seem to be at a close. Now what?

"I spoke with Casey and she says, 'nada, nothing, blanko". It was a professional hit. No casings, no prints, not even an obvious entry point for the shooter into the house. The exit was over the patio. Whoever made the hit, knew exactly how to get in and out without being picked up by the security systems in the neighborhood. They did recover two mashed bullets in a wall painting, but useless."

He placed his J&B back on the bar and turned towards McDonald.

"My guess is it is unlikely we will find out from the crime

scene who or why. This raises the obvious question; where to start?"

"Duncan, do we know who the investigating officer is?"

"Yes, a Lt. Fischer. I don't know him."

"I will make sure you receive a copy of his report and any follow-up filed. Keep seeing Casey in the event she hears something not in the reports."

Duncan looked at McDonald who seemed to be elsewhere in his thoughts.

"What am I missing?"

"Nothing." Replied McDonald.

"Ok, then where do we go from here? We have a dead Central Banker, no apparent motive, no clues at the scene, and a stymied homicide lieutenant."

"I think we can only wait at this point. There has to be another shoe dropping somewhere."

He looked at McDonald and felt something wasn't being said. What other shoe?

"Alan, do you know what this banker's specialty was?"

"Middle East loans and repatriation of frozen assets for some of our friends over there."

CHAPTER 3

LONDON

London hadn't seen real fog since they stopped burning coal for heating of very old, drafty buildings half a century earlier. The loss of fog did not mean an equivalent loss of rain. It was pouring in sheets, barely opaque, when she entered the cab at Heathrow for the West End. Few people were in the streets, as it was a Sunday morning and miserable. The ride past Hammersmith into the center of the West End was as uneventful, as the passport control on entry into the U.K.. For a major world city, it was re-markedly run down, showing only glimpses of a once illustrious past. The elevated highway was an eyesore at best and more often than not, a parking lot to boot.

The Dorchester Hotel remained one of her favorite spots in the U.K. Multiple exits always assured a safe way out; regardless of what chaos might be left by general traffic in and out of the lobby. Her room was old, but bright, with a view of the park. An envelope lay on her nightstand, propped against the reading lamp, addressed to her. It was thick and could wait until after she showered and removed the patina of travel from her hair and skin. The tan acquired in Miami left her looking healthy and attractive against the pasty white women wandering in the hotel in search of something to do. It unfortunately also made her more memorable.

The envelope was thick and heavy. Inside she found a series of photos and a biography of one Nigel Levick. His job title was that of 'Director of Security for the Bank of England'. His photo showed a middle-aged man who had an ex-military air about him. The Bank of England in the City was imposing and suggestive of great strength and moral presence, maintaining the desired effect of her designers. This of course belied all of the pain and suffering, which had been perpetrated by the bank over the many years of its existence. Insiders knew well enough that this institution was the ultimate in the so-called 'old boys' network of the: proper social status, University, and 'The Street'. A very difficult club to gain admittance to, and admittance was jealously guarded by members at all times. Leafing through the bio background, she found a home address in Sussex, a small flat in Kensington, and a club in Pall Mall. Any of the addresses would be adequate and offer sufficient egress once the mark was sent to his maker. Timing would be the issue, as the client wanted termination completed prior to the end of the month. Today was the 20th; not much time left to work. A work schedule was the last piece of information attached to the bio. He would arrive at his office at 8:30 am and leave at 6:00 pm. This never varied, which she needed to check on for herself. His lunch was taken within the confines of the bank. No wife, and no children, but he did have a live-in girlfriend, half his age, named Paula. Weekends were spent playing, when in town, for an over thirty-cricket team in Richmond Park, another good location with plenty of exits, crowds in which to get lost, and constant vehicular traffic in and out of the park's many portals.

She finished dressing and decided to go down to the bar.

Maybe she would get lucky and get some relaxation into a tiring day.

Duncan had spent the last weeks going over the police reports, looking at the crime scene, and contacting every source he had in the D.C. area with no results. It had been frustrating at best. McDonald continued to call for updates that did not exist. Casey as well had not been of help. The killer was gone without a trace. He realized it was now a waiting game to see if anything turned up. Tonight, he had a date with an attractive trial lawyer to the ABA's annual D.C. bash. Normally he avoided these types of venues, however, McDonald had asked him to go, and the trial lawyer was just a bonus.

The Hyatt in Washington was as opulent as the government buildings surrounding it. Taxis coming and going along with a number of limos, for the important and the ones that believed they were important, came and went. His date, Jessica Sierakowski PA, was late. He would have picked her up at her apartment had she not begged off saying late work meant she would meet him there. The night was cold, however, a constant warm breeze passed out through the lobby doors onto the portico area. He watched, as did other passerby's, the constant stream of cars disgorging overdressed, over-made-up, and certainly over bejeweled patrons as they entered the hotel. She arrived fashionably thirty minutes late. Stunning actually in a Versace, full-length evening gown, no jewelry. Jessica could get away with the look. Her five-foot-eight frame, weighing in at 125 pounds in all the right places, made her a standout in any crowd. Her hair was in and out of fashion again, French sweep, with no visible pins holding it in place. Other women glanced in her direction as she came up to Duncan offering her right cheek for a quick kiss.

"Well, you look handsome!"

"Thank you. And you certainly look beautiful. I judge not by my own reaction to that spectacular dress, but the covetous eyes of the women passing you." He grinned as he said it.

"Shall we go in? It is a little chilly out here." She smiled as she said it.

They walked arm in arm up the remainder of the stairs and into the lobby. People in all manner of dress were milling about trying to avoid bumping into one another. One group, obviously here for the ball, moved in the direction of the reception line, while others made haste to leave the area for the lobby bar or elsewhere. It took almost twenty minutes to work their way to a table. Name Tags were visible at individual place settings. They took their seats with a nod to fellow tablemates, all unknown. Duncan looked around the room taking in the gaggle of lawyers, or was it a covey? Between the flashing diamonds, flashing veneered teeth, and overall fake smiles, one could be blinded. In the far corner, he found the odd man out. McDonald was sipping a martini and looking over towards their table. Sometime later in the evening, they would meet as if by chance, while orchestrated by McDonald; a choreography of bodies appearing at random, much like pool balls on a billiard table. Duncan turned back to his date.

"Do you really attend a lot of these rubber chicken events?"

She laughed, but she was also somewhat preoccupied with looking for other attorneys she might know or from her office.

"I go to two or three a year of my own choosing and at least one a month on behalf of the firm."

"You have my sympathies". She laughed. A radiant smile, quick wit, and certainly a beauty to turn heads. He couldn't imagine a better date. She reminded him of Casey.

They spent the next two hours making small talk with fellow tablemates: while lukewarm food, lukewarm wine, and lukewarm platitudes were exchanged. The speeches came and went, followed by dessert. This was at least designed to be cold. Coffee heralded that the evening was rapidly coming to a close. Jessica excused herself for a trip to the lady's room. Duncan looked up at that moment to see McDonald coming towards him.

CHAPTER 4

WASHINGTON

"Having a pleasant evening?" Alan McDonald was not good at social banter. He gestured towards the foyer of the ballroom. Both men walked away from the table.

"I still have nothing." Duncan kept glancing around as he said it.

"We might have a break. The police car, that was second on the scene, had kept his video cam on as he drove to the scene. A car, parked nearby had a female passenger sitting idling as he drove to the victim's house. The car had a Hertz bar code on the side window." McDonald also scanned the room as he said this. No one seemed to be paying them any attention. Most were getting their coats and wraps heading towards the lobby doors one floor away.

"I assume, that was followed up on by the Washington P.D.?" Duncan also kept looking for interest from their fellow guests, while keeping a lookout for Jessica.

"It was. The short answer is we have a picture from the

rental counter where the car was leased. Really a silly mistake on her part, but a break for us."

"Do we have a name?"

"Not yet a real one, but we do know she had a ticket on the Delta flight to Miami under a false name of Mary Wineman. The police are following up on that lead. "

Jessica chose that moment to come outside looking for Duncan. The ballroom was virtually empty, but the foyer still had a number of people chatting about the evening.

"Duncan, did you abandon me?" She smiled as she said it and glanced quizzically at Alan McDonald.

"Jessica, let me introduce you to Alan McDonald, Jessica Sierakowski. Jessica is an attorney with Broad and Lane."

They both shook hands. Alan beamed at the stunning Ms. Sierakowski, wishing he was twenty years younger. Now he was just a dyed-in-the-wool window shopper. His wife liked it that way.

"It is a pleasure to meet you Ms. Sierakowski. I trust you enjoyed the evening with Duncan?"

"Indeed, I did. He kept what is normally a boring evening from sinking to a new low for Washington attorneys." Her eyes danced as she said it. Both Duncan and Jessica knew there could be a future here if they both wanted it. McDonald sensed it as well.

"Thank you. Now if you are both done with the pleasantries, let's get out of here. Alan nice seeing you again."

"Same here Duncan. Give me a call tomorrow and we can continue the conversation." He smiled again at Jessica and left.

"Who is he?" asked Jessica.

"We work together from time to time on freelance assignments I do for the Federal Reserve."

"Is that 'The' Alan McDonald, the man that reports to the President?"

"That's him. He works Security as well. Right now, he is working on some lobbying deal that he wants me involved in. We'll see."

She turned, allowing Duncan to place her wrap over her shoulders. He was still very impressed with how good she really smelled and looked. He also couldn't help noticing others looking at her the same way he did. A successful evening indeed. On the way back to her condominium Duncan was torn between looking at Jessica and wondering why Alan had dropped by at the dinner. A simple phone call would have accomplished the same thing as a so called 'accidental meeting' at an arcane dinner for lawyers.

They arrived back at the condo and rode the elevator to the eleventh floor, where she shared a hall with 1102. Her door was to the right and easily opened with the key she had placed in his hand.

"Get us a drink from the frig. There should be a bottle of Pinot Grigio on the bottom shelf." The night held promise.

"Please unzip me, Duncan."

"My pleasure," He grabbed the top of the gown pressing the zipper ends together and pulling the tab down as far as it would go. THE Bra straps needed freeing as well. He kept a hold of the two ends and pulled Jessica closer to his chest. She let the dress fall to the floor. Carefully he reached around and cupped her breasts gently. She smiled up at him and started to pull towards the bedroom. Duncan followed still holding the bra now free of her. Jessica was indeed beautiful with a smile that could light up any room. Her hair was radiant as ever.

"Well, this certainly falls under Alan's comment about having a pleasant evening. She gave him a light kiss on the cheek as he got up to head to the bath. A shower was in order.

One and a half hours later found Duncan heading out of the building and on his way to his condo. A lot to think about. Jessica was everything a man could want, however, he felt guilty for thinking about Casey as he headed home. Some problems never really go away regardless of any distractions.

This was becoming a problem, as Jessica had feelings, he did not want to hurt her, but so did Casey even if repressed. And from his current feeling as he left Jessica's apartment so did he. A conclusion was definitely in the near future for all three of them. He couldn't just continue to take advantage of Jessica, regardless of how pleasant. It wasn't fair. Thinking about another woman seemed a bad idea, fraught with danger.

Casey was looking at a photomontage taken from multiple cameras near the crime scene. What was shocking was the woman depicted in each picture. She looked Asian, but also very beautiful. The picture showed the driver was concentrating on traffic and unaware of the cameras dotting the cityscape. It was a chance shot by one of the detectives on the scene that brought the pictures to light. Normally they would have gone through all of the footage from traffic cams around the period of the murder.

CHAPTER 5

ANOTHER BANKER DOWN

Instead, this detective had the foresight to review tapes and stills from nearby buildings and traffic cameras both five hours prior and one hour post estimated murder time plus his own car cam. It was unclear if this was indeed the person of interest, however, she was evident in multiple scenes, at multiple times, over the previous three days. More importantly, there was a pile of snow on the roof of her car placing her in the area within two hours of the killing. Not enough driving time had elapsed to have removed the caking on the top of the car.

Casey printed out the pictures and leaned back to look through them again. She might be a local from the same street, but unlikely. This woman would be remembered by anyone who chanced to meet her. Now the question arose, "Who is she?" She reached over to her phone and dialed a colleague in the intelligence unit of the DC Police Department. Maybe he could run a scan of the databases and see what turned up.

It was 18:00 hours. The traffic in the city would be catastrophic with rain, tourists and locals all vying for use of the same streets built over the last four hundred years. There was indeed something to be said for a population culling. He closed his desk, removed all papers from its top, and placed them in a lockable filing cabinet. The outer office was now empty with his secretary having departed some hours ago. Levick picked up his briefcase, grabbed his Mac, and headed for the lift. Getting a cab to Victoria Station and then a train on to Brighton would be hell. His wife had a charity event this evening in 'The Lanes' that would require his dashing home, changing and then on to the event. Tea would consist of poorly cooked chicken, or some Indian concoction that could only be described as mystery meat. There was after all a limit on how much curry could be applied before the details of the meal disappeared in an aromatic haze. Any 'Vindaloo' implied vindictive by association.

As the cab pulled up to Victoria Station, the rain seemed to abate slightly. Thank God for small mercies. He jumped the rivulets of water cascading along the gutter and dashed into the main atrium of the station. Masses of people jostled one another heading to join the exodus of the city. Levick forced his way past a group of American tourists, obviously lost, looking expectantly for help from a non-existent savior. He hurried towards his track hoping to just catch the early express to Brighton. One hour from station to station meant he would be on time for his wife's event. A few tourists were behind him, and a young lady of Asian descent was working her way through the crowd behind him. She lingered long enough to see which track Levick was heading towards and then turned to the ticket counter. A few pounds bought the required passage and she returned to her subject at hand.

Levick found his seat, albeit with difficulty as the car was full of Londoners heading home. It was impossible to see past a few heads of standing-room-only travelers or he would have noticed the beautiful woman with the slightly slanted, cat-like, eyes working her way in his direction. The newspaper on his lap was the Financial Times. The pink sheets were a standard of the paper since its inception and announced to the world an interest in all thing's money. He sensed, rather than felt someone sitting on the seat next to his. A waft of perfume washed over him that reminded of gardenias. Not unpleasant, but somewhat thick for the current atmosphere. He glanced to his left and saw her. She smiled and returned to searching her handbag for some forgotten item yet to be retrieved. The train rattled on, with passengers swaying back and forth as an undulating wave of chaotic motion.

She knew she had the opportunity to finish this now, however, too many people had seen her enter the car and she would be remembered. Still, it had been worthwhile to corroborate the dossiers accuracy on Levicks itinerary. Most of the day had been spent sipping tea across from his office. Boring but essential if the job was to be carried out with minimal disruption. The train pulled to a stop in the station. Both got out. She headed to the 'Lanes' a multiplicity of shops for the well-heeled; he to his home. Nothing more could be gained in following him. She knew now where she would take him and how. She had a week to spare, barring unforeseen complications, a good day all around.

Alan McDonald sat across from the Vice President of the United States, George Allyson. Allyson was an old school republican from Georgia. He had been elected on a platform of 'America First' a slogan taken from Donald Trump. What Allyson had going for him was total trust of the President. The relationship was rare at best, and to some, spooky at worst. The room was otherwise empty and for good reason. Whenever Allyson or the President felt the need to consult with McDonald, it was always alone with no prying eyes, ears, or media people within sight. The Secret Service knew exactly who McDonald was, and did their best to avoid eye contact or recognition of any kind. The relationship between Allyson and McDonald went back decades to their time together at the CIA. Both had moved on, with McDonald becoming a freelance 'fixer' for the country, operating in a maze of bureaucratic tape virtually impenetrable. So many years had passed that the current fleet of media types no longer remembered the McDonald persona. Both men liked it that way; going to great lengths to maintain low profiles when together. Allyson did not know where McDonald maintained an office and also preferred it that way. Plausible deniability. That deniability allowed the executive branch to promote, foster and execute ideas with impunity. Now was not different.

"We have to find out who is behind the assassination of Haughton. It should not be possible with such ease to kill a Federal Reserve executive. How far along are you?"

"I have Innes looking into this now, however he is somewhat stymied as the police have only one clue, a woman, seen at the scene at the right time, and on investigation, she seems to have disappeared on a flight to Miami."

Allyson took another sip from his whiskey and asked, "Do we have a name?"

"No, she traveled under a false name as far as we can tell.

We do have surveillance video from Miami airport that shows she flew to the U.K. a little over a week later. I have informed our friends that she is somewhere in the country, but where is anybody's guess. They have not come back with anything as yet."

"Well keep at it and push Innes a bit."

With that parting shot, Allyson got up and walked out, leaving McDonald to make his own way to the door. One of the Secret Service agents held the door open and seemed to exude an attitude of rather you than me. McDonald just smiled as he passed through. Not the first time that pressure was exerted. He would ignore it as usual and let Duncan get on with it unmolested by political noise.

Levick would exit shortly and take the short walk to the underground; headed for Victoria and then one hour and twenty minutes to Brighton. There was safety in large crowds affording maximum confusion and anonymity. Her hand touched the purse that carried the syringe, pre-loaded. This would suffice to kill a horse, but extremely quick for an adult male.

Levick exited the Bank and started his walk to the underground. She folded her paper, left a small tip, and headed out of the shop, taking up a position well behind Levick. She knew where he was going. There was no hurry. Most passersby barely noticed her as they moved along.

It was one of those London days that came along, rarely. The sun was shining, although slowly sinking in the west. Skyscrapers cast long shadows in the city. She had parked herself in a small café near the exit of the bank. Larger than normal crowds of people clogged the streets, all undoubtedly headed home for tea. The train would be crowed and certainly cramped. Now that she was on the move, it felt better than sitting for an interminable amount of time sipping cold tea. In her handbag was a syringe with enough amber liquid, approximately 10 cc's.

Victoria Station was the usual zoo. Too many people packed in too small a space; all heading home for tea. Over the past twenty years, there had been a trend to move out into the country. This was a boon to small villages, their pubs and local commerce. For sale signs, to let signs, all vied for attention in village after village. Pubs at this time of day would be starting to fill. Publicans would indeed be pleased by the influx of Londoner's piling in for a quick pint before going home. The country was changing; perhaps not for the better.

Levick found his train, and boarded, along with half of Sussex going home. Standing room only was fairly common at this time of day. Commuters pushed and shoved to get a prime spot where holding a rail or strap hangar was easily reached. As the train began to pull out of Victoria, the unnamed young woman hopped onto the first stair and climbed into the adjacent car. She knew many of the passengers would disembark in Red Hill and then disgorge a few more before reaching Brighton. The small prick he felt on his thigh caused him to look around for the source. Only a young woman sat next to him with others standing around the two of them on the moving train. In Red Hill she got off leaving more space for him to spread out a bit. She had looked familiar. He did not make it to Brighton.

As the train pulled into the Brighton Station, so did a variety of police cars and one ambulance. Blue lights flashing, and a series of Bobby's standing at the exit rows. Cameras rolled taking pictures of disembarking passengers. The crush of the crowd passing through narrow turnstiles would help later with the identification from photos taken at the exit. Red Hill had no one greeting the passengers, only a normal flow of people heading home unaware of the now dead body occupying the first-class car. They would read about it in the morning. It was the conductor that raised the alarm.

CHAPTER 6

SAN FRANCISCO

Helen Matsumoto was born in San Francisco in the early nineties. Her family consisted of a grocery store father and a middle school teacher mother. They both were very preoccupied with their jobs leaving the young girl more often than not alone in the two-bedroom apartment. Haight Ashbury was no longer the home of flower power, but rather a run-down, low-income area with a famous name. Many of the apartments were basic walk-ups that had seen better days. While crime was not unheard of, it was more of a home to mild drug users. The police knew it but had bigger fish to fry than bust school kids for smoking grass or the occasional overdose on ecstasy or heroin. It was a diverse neighborhood. Asians, Hispanics, and whites shared the space; along with the patina of dirt and dust on the buildings. Market Street and all of its tourists were just far enough away to not be annoying. The noise from the I-405 could not be thought of the same way. All hours of day and night brought a cacophony of blaring horns, screeching tires, and low rumbles of engines laboring their way in or out of the city.

Her grades were good, if not an A student but, she was known as a loner with no real friends. Still, most teachers appreciated her throughout her school years. No complaints, no behavior problems, virtually invisible. The perfect student. Underneath was a very angry girl. Her parents ignoring her, a school system that assumed she was not there each day, and classmates that remained indifferent to the Asian looking class-mate all forced her further into isolation. As she aged, her inherent beauty began to manifest itself, and with it came boys that suddenly were interested in this quiet young lady. It came too late to shake the scars of her childhood. One senior invited her to the senior prom which she accepted. Her dress was beautiful, and she knew she would stand out at the dance. He unfortunately would not or could not take no for an answer. After the rape, she became cold and distant. The anger had never left her and was now fueled by a need for revenge.

Three days after the incident, she waited for the senior to come home from a late party she knew he had attended. He pulled into his driveway and started to get out of the car. There were no lights in the house as his parents had long since gone to bed. Graduation was scheduled for the morning and he was celebrating his newfound freedom from home, school, and the area in which he lived. Looking up as he exited the vehicle he saw Helen. A smile came across his face.

"Back for a re-do are you?"

"No" she said. He had not seen the gun in her hand; nor did he see the bullet that entered his left eye. For that matter he did not see anything again.

She put the gun back into her bag as the lights came on in the house. Her car was parked around the corner and she walked back to it listening for anyone following. It had been much easier than she expected and satisfying, which she did expect. Since her dad rarely pulled out his gun from his desk drawer, she was sure it would be weeks before he considered cleaning it. By then the cordite smell would be gone. Satisfying indeed!

The police looked for the killer for some months until another case diverted their attention. This one would go into the unsolved murder basket in a city where crimes of this type were not uncommon. Interviews of all of the students and adults that had been friends or schoolmates were conducted. Nothing was found, nor any hint of who, what or why. Evidence that could link the murderer to the murder were not found, and after six months, no one spoke of the matter. The school had taken a day of mourning, offering counseling to students effected, but no one seemed interested. This too passed.

Graduation was uneventful. She had blossomed into a beautiful young woman with a very dark streak well hidden. Her classmates remembered her vaguely, really the boys, but could not tell you anything about her. Likes, dislikes, and boyfriends all vaguely buried in the collective memory. Her sexual awakening came in college, at UCLA where she majored in contemporary English Literature.

Duncan was making his second pot of coffee when his phone rang.

"Her name is Helen Matsumoto. She was born in San Francisco, brought up in Haight Ashbury, post lunatic years of hippies, flower power etc. "

"How did you find her?" Duncan poured his third cup of coffee.

"She was picked up through the Pentagon ID program of past military members, on a facial recognition algorithm. Someone thought to check the picture our young police officer had obtained from the road camera. Couple that one with the rent-a-car service picture and viola! Bob's your uncle." Casey loved being ahead of Duncan. She knew it wouldn't last but for the moment she was the bearer of good news. Now it was Duncan's turn.

"Casey, do you have any good pictures of her? If so, I would like a copy."

"Sure, meet me at DaVinici's at 6 when I get off shift. I'll bring the copies, you buy the wine."

CHAPTER 7

LONDON

"See you then." He hung up and went back to clearing up paperwork that had accumulated over the past month. A necessary evil if he wanted his expenses back from his last job for Alan McDonald. The question would now be how do I track this Helen Matsumoto down.

She was sitting in the lobby bar overlooking the main entrances to the hotel. It was still too early in the afternoon for the rush of office minions to arrive for a quick drink prior to getting on trains for home. Her appointment had been set by encrypted email for 5 pm. This was a first. Her client never met her anywhere, and of course there was always the possibility that he would not turn up today. Communication was always over the net and followed by a packet of the target with appropriate instructions. She had on a light dress, somewhat dark and certainly non-descript. Her concern was not to be too memorable for anyone watching for out-of-the-ordinary patrons. Scanning the room was second nature, however, with so few people frequenting the bar, an overview was easy to maintain. When the older gentlemen with the white hair and grey pin stripped suit came in, she knew he was her contact. A raised hand was enough to have him change course and head over to the table with the rather beautiful Asian girl sipping a gin and tonic.

"Good afternoon, Miss." The accent was pure American, but the attire reeked of English suit makers down to the silk tie. She wondered if he knew his red and yellow stripes represented Cambridge University. Judging by his relative stiffness she guessed he knew.

"Thank you for meeting me on such short notice."

"It is out of the norm. What may I do for you?" She asked while scanning the room yet again for anything out of the ordinary.

"Little point in looking around, you are safe for the time being. I have two men outside of this bar ensuring we will not be disturbed."

A waiter came over and took the drink order glancing at the woman with a raised eyebrow."

"Nothing for me, I am still working on this G and T thank you."

Turning back to the man, she said,

"Why are we meeting now rather than the usual packet?"

"You have been compromised. D.C. has your picture, knows you are in London, and is actively trying to track you down. That is a problem for us and certainly one for you."

It was said quietly, but with a hint of threat. She knew if her persona became common knowledge by law enforcement both the overt and clandestine one, her life span shortened considerably. No government could afford to have such a threat wandering about. The tan kept him from noticing how much she blanched at the news. Outwardly calm, inwardly already planning her escape from the city and the months ahead of recuperation post-plastic surgery. The Asian look would have to go. Epithelial folds around the eyes removed to look more Caucasian, lips made a little thicker and breast size increased from a B-cup to perhaps a C. Hair color was easy and could be handled by a simple trip to the chemists prior to leaving England. The rest would be handled in Brazil which had become the plastic surgery mecca for the world. Expensive, but discreet and far enough off the beaten path to be virtually un-trackable. It had taken her seconds to plan the course of action without losing eye contact with the man across the table from her. The barman returned with his drink order and backed away.

"Do you know who is aware of my existence?"

"Yes. The D.C. Police have your photo from a traffic camera, however the real problem was the rental car. They photograph everyone that comes onto their lot and archive it for one year. That was the opening for backtracking on who you are. From there tracking your flights to Miami and then onto London was child's play."

"I am surprised no one has turned up to arrest me as yet!"

"For all we know, someone may be driving here right now. Our problem is you are a useful asset. Our concern is what happens if you are caught?" The question was asked with a quiet voice, but, the implicit threat was there. If you do not get away, we will have to solve the problem permanently.

"We do not know whom they will send, but I suspect it will not be a policeman. I suggest you leave after this drink and contact us when you are clear and ready to return to work again. We will not be meeting again so there is little point in extending this conversation. This is a warning to be more care-ful. Let us know through existing channels when you are avail-able. I do not want to read about you in the newspaper. Are we clear?"

"We are clear, it will take me 6 to 8 weeks to be ready to

return. Please keep me informed on who is looking and the status of their investigation."

She got up, put down a five-pound note for her drink, and left the bar. Turning left, she exited the hotel with just her handbag and a light coat. She would not be going back to her room, nor attempt to recover any of her belongings. The game had changed; she was on her own. A red cab, the new look of London taxis was in the taxi rank. She entered the cab and directed it to Heathrow Airport. At the same moment, she entered the cab, Innes entered the lobby through the same doors she had departed. He headed towards the lobby reception area unaware of how close they had missed one another.

Innes registered under his real name, got his key, and moved to the lift for his room. A casual glance around the hotel lobby and through the glass door towards the lobby bar revealed no one of interest. One patron in a dark suit was paying his bill and appeared ready to leave. No one else occupied any of the visible seats. Duncan waited patiently for the lift and when it arrived he got in heading towards the fifth floor. The visit with Casey had been productive. The pictures the D.C. police had been able to collect would help for at least the short term. There was little doubt Helen Matsumoto would change her appearance. Whether the change was sufficient to fool facial recognition software at major airports was to be seen.

He thought back to the meeting with Casey. It was always a pleasure seeing her even if on occasion a bit of awkwardness entered into the conversation. They discussed current significant others, work and of course the findings of the D.C. special ops unit. Helen Matsumoto was considered a real threat and was being actively pursued now by a variety of agencies. Her good luck came down to the government's inability to share knowledge across multiple platforms and an inbred jealousy-guarding capabilities as well as data sharing. As far as D.C.

knew, the last and only lead was in London. Now that he was here, it appeared less and less likely that MI-5 could be of help. After a quick shower and shave from the long flight, Duncan dressed and went back down to the lobby. He started again towards the bar, but it was empty. A quick walk across the lobby brought him up to the front desk.

"May I help you?" The concierge looked over his computer at the tall American before him.

"Just a quick question." Duncan fished the picture out of his jacket and placed it face up on the counter.

"Have you seen my niece here today? She was traveling out of London but should be back." He smiled as he said it looking directly at the man in front of him. No threat, just a friendly question.

"Well, normally I would not be able to answer that question, but as it is your niece, I saw her leave the hotel about one hour ago. She seemed in a hurry."

"Oh, that's a surprise. We were supposed to have dinner here tonight. May I leave a message for her?

"Certainly sir, what should I say?"

"Please tell her I am in the lobby bar and I will wait there for her."

"And your name sir?"

"Duncan in room 715."

The concierge was writing this diligently down and putting it into an old fashioned pigeon box behind him where keys hung. Room 412 did not show a key, yet the concierge had seen her leave the hotel. Duncan turned away with a thank you, heading towards the bar. The lobby was getting more crowded and a few had drifted into the bar as he reached it. A quick scan showed she was not in the room. If Matsumoto had gone out of the hotel, she left with her key. It was now a waiting game.

Heathrow was busy as always. Between travelers milling about in search of the proper check-in kiosk and police, well armored and armed, room to move was at a premium. The police did not appear to be looking for anyone in particular, however, they did glance at all that passed through their view. She looked around her as she passed a pair of them, neither looking directly at them nor away that might cause suspicion. Police were trained to observe certain types of behavior that warranted another closer look. The pretty girl walking by did not fall into that category.

The Aeroflot kiosk was in front of her. Her passport read Yuko Ito. She was a student at Moscow University, studying Economics. The new semester would start shortly so she was returning to school. The desk agent printed out an aisle seat economy boarding pass and checked her luggage.

"Have a nice flight miss."

"Thank you". No more needed to be said as the agent already was beckoning the next passenger behind her to come forward. Anonymity had real value. Passport control was perfunctory, and she passed through with no concerns. Her makeup, hair color change, and glasses were just enough to pass the facial recognition profile, but she knew it wouldn't hold up forever. Eventually, the tapes would be analyzed by ever-increasing software sophistication until she was discovered having taken the flight to Moscow. The trip to Caracas would require three more flights, two long drives with a commandeered vehicle, and a series of makeup, hair color, and weight changes. By the time she was on a flight from Cairo to Caracas, five days would have passed having created an impossible task for any pursuer.

Duncan sat at his kitchen table reading mail that had arrived since his visit to London. That had been a total waste of time. Hours spent in the Hotel, a short trip to her room finding clothes but nothing else, and then back to D.C. to look for answers. She had been tipped off that someone was looking for her and just left. The mail held nothing of interest and the newspaper he had picked up on arrival at JFK was even less interesting. The death of Levick in Brighton was already reduced to page three, soon to be a snippet in the Obit column, and then gone.

"Casey was helpful with the picture and general description, but I still missed her in London. Apparently by just a few minutes." Duncan refilled his coffee cup.

McDonald said, "Well that can't be helped. She still however is a priority."

"I assume she left the country and now is in the wind."

"You'll have to wait and see if anything turns up. We have people watching all of the obvious places, but I believe, since she left so abruptly, that she was tipped off. We are working on that now, but if she went East it will be hard to track her."

Duncan nodded to himself, and then said "She is very good at her job. The camera mistakes were lucky for us. It might take a while for her to resurface."

There was silence for what seemed like minutes. Duncan waited, no point in filling space while McDonald thought about the next move.

"There is another bit of news for you. Apparently, our young Helen was busy in London."

"Yes?"

"She appears to have taken out one Nigel Levick, the Director of Security at the Bank of England. Of course, the question arises what does our Nigel have to do with Federal Reserve Banker?"

Innes responded with "it can't be a coincidence. Both working for major banks, albeit in very different capacities."

"I agree, but again cameras at the train station picked her up getting on the train to Brighton right behind our Mr. Levick. We are looking for a connection." McDonald said his goodbyes and returned to his office desk to resume his normal activities. Duncan called Casey to arrange where they could have dinner that night. There were questions.

Levicks comment of 'it might take a while' was an understatement. No news is good news, but, Duncan knew she was out there somewhere and she would resurface. Her job skills, while laudatory, were limited in scope. The only thing for it was to wait and see when the next penny dropped.

He placed the call to Casey.

"How about a drinks and dinner tonight, same place?"

CHAPTER 8

―――――

FLIGHT

"See you there," she said and hung up. Jessica was out of town on depositions for some large client, so he was on his own. Normally that meant extra workout time, and more research into the latest target, Helen Matsumoto, but perhaps seeing Casey would bring new information.

Casey had spent the day answering calls from just about every division within Metro DC's area. It was exhausting to hear the same issues again and again, but she had been part of the homicide task force for over a year and it still required listening to inane requests for help when local agencies could deal with local homicides. Dinner and drinks tonight with Duncan sounded like fun. She was after all filled with curiosity on how far he was with the banker's murder. So far, DC police had come up with nada. A photo of the possible suspect and obvious alias used to rent a car all meant little without the woman being in custody. As an afterthought, she made a quick call to a friend in records to see if something new on the woman turned up.

"Nothing here, other than a lid has been put on the case."

The voice was that of Jeannie a friend who often shared information she shouldn't. They just liked each other and Casey knew Jeannie wanted her to climb the ladder to becoming a captain or higher. Rather like a den mother, only younger.

"Any idea why the 'lid' and who put it on?"

"Why, no idea. The lid belongs to the Commissioners office. It is therefore political or he wouldn't have become involved."

"Thanks Jeannie. Still looking at this case as an outsider."

"Be careful Casey. If the Commissioner is involved this might be a hot case not worth following. Drop by for coffee when you get a chance. Things are quiet here".

"Will do, and thanks."

The Asian girl was no more! Her appearance had changed subtly from the surgeon's point of view, however drastically from any camera shots that might exist. Her epithelial folds around the eyes were gone. Contact lenses had changed her eyes from brown to blue. Her hair was now auburn, not too red, but enough to change the overall impression. She had lost some additional weight, and being slight to begin with gave her a slightly emaciated look. That would change once she was eating again. Her bags were packed and ready to go. A floral print dress, matching shoes, and a handbag completed the picture of an international traveler. The first test of course would be entering into the United States in Los Angeles. The concern would be facial recognition systems at the airport. If she passed those without incident, she was safe. The added fat tissue on her cheekbones, while slight would throw the algorithm off, or so she hoped. Once in L.A. a short taxi ride to Marina Del Rey and she would be virtually hidden among the beautiful people. Her passport was now in the name of Caryn Taylor, addressed in the Marina. Social Security numbers, driver's licenses had all been arranged by her employer. In short, no comebacks from any curious inspection at the airport or traffic stop by an overzealous official. Her apartment was on the first floor of a third-floor building. Each apartment overlooked the marina, with one million-dollar yachts riding the moving water. The creaking was annoying to the non-sailors, however most residents got used to the sound very quickly.

Chapter 9

Brazil

She tossed her handbag on the sofa and pulled her suitcase into the bedroom. A shower and a few hours of sleep were in order after the fourteen hours of travel from Rio. She knew she had to report in as soon as possible, but a shower came first. Time enough afterward to reconnect and see if there were any additional tasks for her to complete.

Washington had become considerably quieter since Helen Matsumoto had visited. Spring was starting to show signs of life. Since no murders had occurred, or at least one's that came to Alan McDonald attention, Duncan was left with little to do. Housekeeping chores of expenses, billing etc. were items that needed attention. His exercise program continued, but even Casey and Jessica had fallen off the screen. Casey was busy working on her Lieutenants exam. Jessica was in Washington doing depositions for her firm. It almost felt like summer.

Duncan walked down to a deli near his building for a quick breakfast. On entering he saw most of the tables were still empty. An orange juice, bagel with cream cheese and lox (a habit acquired during his stay in New York City), and black coffee were as good a start to the day as any other. The waitress, by mutual consent as a regular customer, flirted a bit and then left him to his breakfast. The timing was everything. The last bite of the bagel had hardly been washed down by the coffee when the phone rang.

"Duncan, Alan. We are starting to see political pressure to let the Asian girl just drop off our person of interest list" "How do you know?"

"The VP gave me a call and said that it might be a good idea to stop rattling cages. This of course is what I have been doing the past three months. Nothing, until Allyson called. Now, I want to know why."

The pause didn't last long.

"Let me check again with Casey and see what she has. I'll call you back in half an hour if I can reach her." They both hung up. Duncan stood up, put $20 on the table, waved good-bye, and went out to the street. Foot traffic was building as the morning rush not to be late reached its peak. Duncan pulled out his cell phone and called Casey while keeping up with everyone milling about him. It rang five times prior to a pickup.

"Hi, Duncan. What's up?"

"Just checking in. Anything new on Helen Matsumoto?"

"Not really, but I did have an interesting conversation a few weeks ago with a friend in records. She said that a lid has been put on all information about Matsumoto without clearance from the commissioner."

Duncan thought about that a moment and was interrupted by Casey.

"Are you still there?"

"Yes, just thinking, why would anyone from the Commissioner's office shut the information flow down? Any leads from your end?"

"No Duncan, but I can check with Lt. Fischer and see if he is still active on the case."

"Ok, thanks. Call me back if you get anything."

CHAPTER 10

LONDON TO MOSCOW

No new news had come in the past few weeks relative to the Asian girl and it appeared as if this was now on the back burner. Even Alan McDonald had chosen not to contact Duncan for any new problems or updates. Still, he wondered what had become of her. They had tracked her down to a flight from London to Moscow but then lost her to the antiquated computer systems available in Russia. At this point, she could be anywhere in the world. No new bankers had shown up dead, nor anyone else on McDonald's radar.

Casey's apartment was best described as spartan. It was an old loft that had been a storage area for cotton bales in another era. The entrance consisted of a freight elevator that could only be operated by a key. The entrance was a small vestibule at street level with a door to the left allowing access to the lower storage level. At the time unoccupied. The was an air of dust throughout the lower level that quickly disappeared on reaching her third-floor entry way. The apartment was over 3000 sq. feet divided into separate areas by plants. No walls, plenty of pipes and walls of brick. A large bedroom area housing a king-size mattress on a low-slung frame, two side tables with lamps and a runner on the floor to one side of the frame. A dresser with brass handles added to the minimalist look. The one concession to a room was the bath area. Large claw foot, turn of the century, tub dominated the area, while a small sink, vanity, and mirror rounded out the rest coupled with a toilet. The latter was an antique with a gravity feed, chain pull flush apparatus. The living room, if one could call it that, had a small TV, sofa, and two lazy boy recliners visible. A long seaman's trunk served as a coffee table and subbed as a storage area. At first glance no one would believe this was a woman's home. Industrial string lighting ran the length of the apartment. They were dimmable but would have caused some concern with their bare wire connectors.

Casey liked its utilitarian design. It was easy to clean, and although austere, it would hardly be targeted by burglars seeking high-end pickings. As she poured her third cup of coffee the phone rang. She was off for the weekend and didn't expect anyone other than a robo-caller to reach out.

"Hello"

"Hi Casey. This is Lt. Fischer from metro homicide. Gotta minute?"

Duncan's project seemed to be spilling yet again over onto her.

"Sure, what can I do for you?" she replied.

"You know a Duncan Innes or?"

"I do, why?"

"I would like to meet him. His name keeps coming up in my homicide investigation." There was a pause prior to her answering.

"You might want to ignore that. He is one of the good guys and very well connected." She knew that wasn't enough to satisfy him, but worth a try.

"I understand, but I still want a word."

She thought for a minute and then said,

"Let me call him and ask him to call you. Believe me, it is easier that way."

"Fine, but tell him it is important." He hung up.

Casey thought about it for a few minutes prior to dialing. Duncan would not be pleased to be asked to call the homicide officer. He worked below the radar and never wanted to be seen or heard of by anyone in the public arena including the police.

On the third ring, she heard,

"Hi Casey, what's up?"

"I just got a strange call from Lt. Fischer, DC Homicide asking for your number. I didn't give it; however, I am sure I will hear about that. He wants you to call him. Something about the murder he is working on where your name came up. Sorry to ask this, but it will be easier all the way around if you just call him. Otherwise, my chain of command will start leaning on me."

Duncan was silent for a few moments.

"Duncan, are you still there?"

"Yes, just thinking how my name came up."

"I do not know, just call him and let me know what happened please."

She gave him the direct line to Fischer and after a few parting words about a future dinner hung up. Something not good was up and she did not want to be involved. Duncan was a big boy and could take care of himself.

Duncan rarely interacted with the police department and never during a high-profile homicide investigation. There could be no logical reason for his name to come up with this homicide detective unless there was a connection, he was unaware of between the victim and himself.

"Lt. Fischer, this Duncan Innes, I was told you wanted to speak with me?"

"Yes, Mr. Innes."

"Duncan is fine. I understand you know Casey? A good cop and a close friend." Emphasis on the friend part.

"Indeed, I did ask her to have you call. Just a few questions. Do you have the time now or could we meet over coffee?"

Duncan thought about this for a few seconds. He was largely unknown by the D.C. Police and didn't really want to change that; however, a meeting might gain information that Alan McDonald had as yet not passed on.

"Sure, where and when?"

Fischer offered a Starbucks near the central Police Department and a choice of times.

"Three PM works for me. Do I need to bring my lawyer?"

Fischer laughed.

"If you needed a lawyer, I would have just picked you up and brought you here. No need, just a few questions. I am sure that Casey told you it was about the Central Bankers murder?"

"She did, however, I am not sure how I am involved or of interest to you?" No answer was coming forth. They agreed to a 10 am meeting at the central police station, rather than the Starbucks offered.

Lt. Fischer had spent the past few hours trying to understand just who Duncan Innes actually was. Who did he really work for all he had was a freelance consultant with a very nice address in Central D.C.. Whether Innes could offer him anything of value in the murder investigation remained to be seen. As he put away the file the phone rang showing it was an internal number. Innes had arrived.

"Good day, Mr. Innes. I appreciate you coming down on such short notice"

"Casey said I should come, makes everyone's life a little easier.'

Fisher shuffled some papers before him and then glanced back up to Duncan. It was a very short meeting. Duncan's phone rang before he could answer any questions.

'Sorry Lt. Fisher, but that was Alan McDonald asking for a meeting. When he calls, I answer. If you have specific questions, email me, the address is on the card I gave you. I will try and answer, but for the moment there is nothing I can do to help you. I am just not involved in this. If that changes, I will get back to you. Sorry, but I really must leave now. On the way out Duncan could feel Lt. Fishers eyes following him out. This was too close to the local police for his tastes, but somehow his name had come up. Why? He half thought that he would run into Casey, but found himself on the street without seeing her. Not the ideal place to meet ex-girlfriends. His phone rang again.

"Hi, Alan. Just leaving the Police Station. See you in a few minutes."

The cab ride to Alan's office was short and uneventful. Not always the case with the preponderance of foreign drivers. Every one of them seemed to be a student for an advanced degree in a local University. Their driving skills were directly proportionate to their language ones. Regular crashes were the norm in D.C., although today's trip passed accident-free. The weather was warm so there were many pedestrians out and about. None paid any attention to the cab and the departing guest. The office building was typical Washington non-descript. Fake façade with the same nondescript receptionist in the front window.

Alan's office was on the 12th floor. Mirrors on every floor kept the complaints of riders to a minimum on wait time. They were too busy looking at themselves to realize how long a wait was at hand for the next elevator to arrive. Duncan got on board with two others and they were off to the 12th. Both men ignored Duncan on the ride up. They kept their eyes fixed on the flashing numbers showing which floor they were passing. One had a somewhat slovenly appearance. Badly in need of a shave and seemed out of place in this building. When the ding indicating they had arrived on the 12th floor chimed both stood directly in front of the opening door. Duncan remained in the back of the cage and only slowly got off as the other two headed out and to the right towards the Suite marked Alan McDonald ESQ.. Duncan's problem radar was dinging madly. He never ignored any subliminal messages when it came to his own safety; which had saved him many times in the past. The larger of the two men entered the office without looking around for his partner. The other turned back towards Duncan and was met by a roundhouse of a punch administered by someone who knew how. He folded and went to the floor. He would be out of it for a few minutes. The other entered the offices and turned to the receptionist, completely unaware of what had just happened to his partner. Duncan did a quick pat down removing the snub-nosed 38 pistol and pocketing it. He rarely carried any type of arms in D.C. Too much bother if he accidentally ran into a police check. Hard to explain the carry. Sometimes he felt with the high murder rate and mugging that the city should be handing out arms to visitors in case they had none. A cynical position in any case. Time to get into McDonald's office. On entering he saw the receptionist staring at the entranceway to Alan's office. She nodded to Duncan towards the door. There was an air of concern about her. He moved to the door while scanning the waiting room. No one else was present. The thick carpeting kept his movement extremely quiet. The door was ajar allowing him to hear two people speaking in the inner office. One was McDonald's; the other had to be partner number two. He pulled the pistol of the now K.O.ed other and entered. McDonald looked up at him having caught the movement in his peripheral vision. That in turn triggered the man's attention who also turned and looked. As he moved his right hand came out of his pocket holding another gun like his partner's. Before he could react to this new threat, Duncan opened fire with two shots. One to the abdomen, being the largest target, and one to the shoulder, although Duncan had tried for the heart. Precision shooting was only possible in the movies. His job was to mitigate the threat and protect McDonald's.

"How did you know?" said McDonald."

CHAPTER 11

WASHINGTON

"I rode up with them in the elevator. His partner is outside cold-cocked, you might call the cops please." McDonald started to dial 911 and looked at Duncan and then at the body on the floor. You have made a mess of my new carpeting Duncan!"

"You're welcome, Alan. At least it is not my blood nor yours, or?"

"' Now who are they, Alan?"

" I do not know but will find out. You may want to secure the guy outside. The police should be here shortly."

A prophetic comment. They could hear the cops questioning the receptionist. Alan opened his door to the receptionist area. Two policemen in uniform stood in front of the receptionist's desk.

"Gentlemen, do come in. This is Duncan Innes who is contracted to this office for protection if and when needed. I am Alan McDonald. "

The older policeman stated "Do not touch anything on the one, you or he shot. I will take a statement in the meantime. I have ordered an ambulance for this one and the one in the hall. He has a broken jaw from his outward appearance and cannot talk. This one seems much worse for wear. Which one of you shot him?"

"I did officer, when I came into the office, he turned to me with a gun in his hand. I was a little faster."

" You certainly were. Any idea of who this is?" The questioner did not seem to expect an answer.

Duncan looked at Alan McDonald, who studiously looked at the policemen. "We have no idea, but their accent suggested a Brit. The one in the hall did not speak, nor apparently cannot anyway. Perhaps you two can shed light on this?"

"We will have to wait for the Detectives to arrive. Should just be a few minutes, as we are still downtown. "

Casey arrived a little out of breath.

'Either one of you injured or hurt?"

She looked at Duncan and then towards Alan McDonald. "We are both good Casey, but this one on the floor is no longer with us and the one in the hall seems worse for wear."

Casey nodded and pulled out her notebook. She started making notes knowing full well that Duncan was the one that had pulled the trigger on the occupant laying on the Floor.

"Do either of you know the victims?" A uniform 'no' was uttered.

She then began the process of getting both their accounts of the two assailants. The one in the hall was moaning when the ambulance EMTs' arrived. He was quickly bundled onto a stretcher and then moved to the elevator.

"Casey, I would like to have a word with the one in the hall, before he is taken away."

"Not going to happen. Since you were the one that broke his jaw, I can't allow you to speak with him. We need his statement first since the other here cannot speak for himself. I will get you both a copy of the coroners' report, identity, etc. if found. In the meanwhile, our police photographer has arrived and he needs to take photos of the scene before we move the body.

"Well then, how about dinner tonight?" Duncan says it loud enough for her to hear but not the other officer in the adjacent room.

"What about Jessica?"

"She is out of town doing her lawyer thing. Back the end of next week."

'Sure, why not? Where should we meet?"

"How about LA PERLA on Pennsylvania at 8 pm?"

"See you then Duncan."

Duncan made the reservation and left his home at 7 pm on his way to the restaurant. He was careful to look around at his environment as he walked. It was only a few blocks, but better to be careful. Once there he looked around for Casey, but he was early. He ordered a nice Barolo and a bottle of sparkling water. The Restaurant was still relatively empty but that would change in the next hour.

His cell phone suddenly began to vibrate. Taking a quick look, he saw it was a White House number. Not often that he received calls from the White House, but at least he knew it would be secure.

"Duncan Innes here, what can I do for you?"

The voice on the other end came on and said this is a call from the Vice President's office.

"What can I do for you?" At that moment he saw Casey coming towards his table. He waived her to a chair while holding his cell. She still was beautiful even though the call was a distraction.

"The Vice President would like to meet with you tomorrow morning if you are available. Would 10 am work for you?"

"Blair House or the White House?" Duncan said it loud enough for Casey to hear. Her eyebrows raised quizzically.

"The White House please, your name and time will be at the main entrance." They both hung up.

" And, what was that all about?" Casey smiled at Duncan. After all, it was not every day that your date was invited to the White house.

'Your guess is as good as mine. I have had very little contact with George Allyson. In fact, I have only met him twice. Very short meet and greet type meetings. Each one occurred last year and together with Alan McDonald. I do have to call Alan to see what he knows. It can wait till I get home though"

He took a sip of the wonderful Barolo now aerating at the table. Casey also raised her glass. Duncan watched her drink; thinking why they were not together any longer. She was indeed beautiful, smart, and a great companion.

Duncan's phone rang, at the moment he was paying the dinner bill.

"Hi Alan, what's up?"

" I just heard you are invited to the White House tomorrow!"

""Yes, any idea what that is about and how did you hear of this so fast? I was about to call you"

Duncan held his hand up to keep Casey at bay.

The dinner had been fun, however, the cloud of why the sudden meeting with the Vice-President cast a bit of a downer for the evening. Too many questions with no answers.

CHAPTER 12

THE WHITE HOUSE

Duncan arrived on time and was escorted to a waiting area in a non-descript hallway where Alan McDonald was seated on a sofa waiting to be summoned.

"You too?" Duncan took a seat next to Alan. Both looked at the Secret Service men standing in front of a nearby door.

"Any ideas on why we are here?"

McDonald responded with a shrug.

'They both recognized the young lady that came out from behind the double doors. One thing was certain, the V.P. did have a good eye for assistants.

"This way gentlemen." She led them through the entrance and into an obvious conference room. Small mahogany table, 6 chairs. The V.P. was as yet not there.

"Can I get coffee for either of you?"

"Yes, please black, no sugar."

Alan asked for one lump and some cream. The game was played in Washington by a known set of rules. If you were important the V.P. would have been waiting. However, the farther down the Totem pole you were determined the wait time. Both Alan and Duncan had played many times. As they looked at one another with a half grin on their faces, the doors opened again. Both stood out of respect for the office if not the man. The V.P. walked in with two Secret Service men close behind.

"Sorry for keeping you waiting, but I had to finish up something, which took a little longer than planned."

Both men nodded. Been there, done that.

'Well, Mr. Vice President, what can we do for you?"

Duncan took a sip of his coffee. He watched the Secret Service men in the room doing their job of protecting the V.P., eyes constantly scanning looking for threats.

Alan looked on expectantly at the V.P. fully aware that Duncan was also scanning the room. Everyone seemed a little tense without cause. For Duncan, that was the normal state of affairs.

" I asked you both to come by as I wanted an update on the status of your investigation into the two bankers' deaths. I recognize one was security and IT in the U.K., but the other was a friend. Anything new here?"

Alan responded although he looked uncomfortable.

'So far just a blank. We believe it was a woman that caused both deaths; however, that is not confirmed fully."

"Well please keep me informed."

Duncan spoke up first.

"Sir, this is an internal investigation. Why do you care?"

Alan looked over to him with a bit of 'why did you ask that' look on his face.

The Vice President gave away nothing.

" My interest is personal. Mr. Haughton was a friend of mine. Are we any closer to finding out what, who etc., and why he was murdered" The Vice President looked at Alan and Duncan, clearly expecting an answer.

Duncan replied first

'No sir, we know the killer was a woman or at least it looks that way."

"Any leads as yet?"

"No sir, however, we did track her down to a London hotel, but I just missed her by about 30 minutes."

The V.P. looked a bit chagrined, however, just nodded.

"Well, keep me informed on progress. Call me at any time. Either, you Alan, or You, Duncan. I can be reached at any time." With that, he stood up. Indicating the meeting was over and nothing more would be added. Both Duncan and Alan rose with him and followed through the door by which they came into the room.

Both men entered the limo and were whisked off to Alans' office block. The police cars were still there but looked more like protection than crime scene officers. The crime was now a day old, hardly necessary for their presence.

" Save the questions for my office." Alan had headed off the obvious question.

CHAPTER 13

THE APARTMENT

They parked in underground parking, with Duncan doing a quick sweep through the bays. He wasn't looking for anything specifically, but anything out of place. He found it on the second look-through. A large bag had been left by one of the cars in bay 16. He was now about 100 feet away from the bag. They had parked in bay 2 which was about 150 feet away. Better than closer, but still too near. Before he could finish the thought and evaluate the threat, the bag exploded sending car parts, and shrapnel throughout the garage. Duncan was hit once, a miracle in itself, it was just a graze on his left arm. The car next to the bag was demolished. The roof of the garage had also seen better days. An acrid pall of smoke was in the air. The bleeding from his am was insignificant but needed attention regardless. It had just become personal. Duncan had seen enough IEDs in Iraq, to not want to see anymore. Still, he knew he was lucky. Had he continued to do his walk around; the bomb would have shredded him. The difference between life and death was just few feet.

"Alan are you O.K.?" the sounds of sirens became audible.

The sprinkler fire system had come on with the explosion. Now everything was wet and getting wetter. Small puddles of water reflected the flashing red lights of the fire truck arriving through the main gated entrance. The police were right behind it.

"I am fine. Some damage to the rear of the limo, but other than that, all good. What about you, you seem to be bleeding?"

Duncan looked at his arm, which had finally stopped leaking. It was clotting off and although it hurt, nothing major. 'Let's get up to your office, get a dressing on it and I am good to go." Duncan wanted to be out of the area as quickly as possible. There could be a second device.

The Fire Marshall walked over and asked what had happened.

"Satchel bomb went off, too late. Just missed." Alan took Duncan by the arm and headed towards the elevators.

Forty-five minutes later a bandage was in place and the police arrived and were busy in the hall with Alan's secretary. Fire Marshall in tow.

" You two are keeping this department busy these days. First the attempted murder, now a bomb in an office garage. You must have annoyed someone." He said it like a question.

Duncan responded with "Not half as annoyed as I am right now."

" We will find out who planted the bomb. But, for the moment, let's go back to the V.P. meeting this morning. Why did he call for this meeting?" Duncan waited for a response from Alan.

"I really cannot say. The president had tasked the V.P. with keeping an eye on The Iranians, nothing else. There is a lot of movement there between Iran and Syria. The president does not want to be caught by surprise. With Hamas in Israel and the nonsense in Yemen, things are heating up. the VP is supposed to be the expert with his ties to the Middle East. I do not know what the connections to the Bankers are?"

The police continued to ask who might have placed the bomb. Neither Alan nor Duncan had any ideas. They referred back to the two thugs that had visited Alan's office earlier. So far, no leads on that end either, but both believe it had something to do with the bankers' death and subsequent investigation. A lot of people were asking questions. Not only the local police but also all of Alan's contacts were nosing around. Some rock had been turned over. But two attempted killings seemed excessive.

"Duncan, I do not know why the V.P. called the meeting. I do know he knew Haughton from the Federal Reserve. They had been at University together from what I'm told. I suspect he was indeed a friend. Beyond that, it does seem odd. I am trying to get a read from the President."

Duncan responded "Let me know what you hear. I am going back to my apartment. I need a shower and a change of clothes. I'll call you tonight unless you have something earlier."

Duncan took the elevator back to the lobby. He was preparing to get out when the doors opened. Two men were standing in front of the entrance. Both did not look like they belonged. The first pulled a gun from the inside of his jacket and started to point it at Duncan. The other looked over his shoulder towards the main entrance. Duncan took one step out of the cage reaching forward with his right hand and wrapping his fingers around the barrel of the gun. With his left hand, he swung it around toward the forearm of the gunman pushing it in the opposite direction to his right hand now traveling quickly to his left. The gun came loose. Otherwise, the gunman would have had a broken hand. The gun was now in Duncan's right hand and came up to the face of the prior holder. The other man turned towards Duncan and pulled out his gun. Duncan was quicker firing over the right shoulder of the first assailant. Number two dropped to the floor with a bullet in his head. He was dead before he hit the ground. The building would be very unhappy with the cleaning bill.

"Your partner is no more. Take a seat over there and give me your wallet." He waved the gun in the direction of the lobby chairs. Number one started in that direction.

"Don't even think about turning around towards me or you join your partner."

Duncan took the proffered wallet and looked at the driver's license. Harvey Landau, address in the Pentagon City area of D.C. Very odd address for a would-be killer.

"Who sent you?" There was no response. Duncan pulled out his cell phone and dialed Alan. It was answered on the first ring.

"I'm in the lobby, call the cops, I just shot one character and am holding the other in the lobby. They seemed intent on shooting me. I am really getting a bit tired of these constant attempts on you and me."

'I'll call, but from the sounds of it, they are already here. One of the neighbors or other offices must have called the gunshots in, take care. The D.C. cops are a little tense right now."

Fortunately for Duncan, the first policeman through the door was Casey. She immediately removed her cuffs from her belt and put them on the sitting man in front of Duncan.

"We have been busy again." Casey wasn't smiling.

The man squirmed a bit, but Casey kept him quiet.

"I strongly suggest you remain seated and quiet."

Two other officers came through the lobby entrance. Immediately they converged on the cuffed man sitting in front of Casey. Casey re-holstered her service weapon, a Glock

"What have we here?" said the first officer. Casey filled him in with what Duncan had told her.

'He's all yours. Attempted murder of Mr. Innes here, who I know personally and is a friend of the President. I will take his statement, but run this idiot in and book him for me please, Attempted murder, etc. I will be down to the station in about an hour. The Coroner is on his way. He is also bringing a bus for the body."

The two uniforms left with the suspect.

"This is worse than dating you. The only time I see you now is when someone is trying to kill you."

"Sorry Casey, not something I wanted." Casey looked exasperated.

"How does Jessica deal with this?"

Duncan shrugged his shoulders.

"You do realize I can't cover for you forever?" She showed her concern for the near miss but also intimated that Alan McDonald was going to have to intervene.

"Do you want to go and get some coffee?"

"I would love to Casey. In answer to your Jessica question, she never seems to notice that I am being shot at, etc. regularly." He laughed as he said it, but also realized by verbalizing it, he had his answer on any long-term relationship.

"Can you drop me off at my place, please? My Arm seems to be hurting and we used Alan's limo to get here.

"Sure we D.C. cops love to serve. The cruiser is outside. Look before you cross the street." Not funny, but sage advice.

Thirty minutes later, Duncan was entering his condo carefully with a walk around to ensure no surprises. Casey followed also looking for anything out of place. She had been here many times before. Everything looked in order. The condo was empty of any visible threats. Better to err on the side of caution than to pick up body parts in the future, especially her own.

"Why do you think you keep being targeted?"

"No good answer. We are not even close to the killer of the Banker or the IT guy in London. We do suspect a woman. She has disappeared. If the crimes are related, no one has told me how. We have established that the two knew each other from a previous Bankers meeting. How Alan found that out is beyond me, but it is known now. The meetings may have been casual. Still working on that."

Casey came back into the living room.

"Well, I can't find anything in the apartment at this time. Just be careful Duncan. Life would be boring without you and I hate funerals."

"I'll try to avoid one, at least mine. Want to stay for dinner? I can make something from the fridge."

" No thanks, I have to get back to the station, do my report, and ensure that Alan has you covered. Call me tomorrow if you need anything. For a change, try not to kill anyone today. I dislike all the paperwork and explanations that result from your activities."

As Casey started to leave, the phone rang.

"Hi Alan, anything new?:

"Yes, Duncan. It would appear that I was not the target of the last bomb in the garage. That only leaves you, so be careful. I got a call from Blair House and they said Intelligence picked up chatter that you are to be eliminated. You are now a target. Who have you annoyed?"

CHAPTER 14

THE OFFICE

"No idea, Alan. The only thing I know is a woman is behind the assassinations, you have all of that information. The V.P. does as well, as far as I know. Casey is the one that produced that info."

The conversation continued for five minutes and then Alan hung up. Duncan was left with white noise from the phone. He was very annoyed.

Whoever wanted him dead made the first and second mistakes by being unsuccessful on two tries. It is indeed time to be a little more aggressive. The D.C. cops would not let him interrogate the suspects. The next one, would not be going to the police if another try was attempted. Enough was enough. Duncan washed out the wine glass that Casey had used and his scotch glass as well. He had to make himself a visible target to lure out the next victim. This brought him to the idea of going back to the bar that he and Alan had previously used as a meeting point, The Whale. Traffic was light. He arrived just before 6 pm, still happy hour. One of those misnomers as the customers always seemed more desperate than happy. The usual crowd of suits stood by the bar. There was a cacophony of sound from the bar area, including false laughter. Duncan made his way to an empty spot and beckoned the bartender over to him.

'Just a J&B with soda and a little ice."

The bartender took off immediately to get the drink. He had recognized Duncan from his previous visit. Alan was always a good tipper which ensured continuing good service. As the drink arrived so did a beautiful young lady. She was small compared to Duncan, but well put together. He smiled at her, and was met with a wider smile in reciprocation.

"Hi, aren't you a little big for that bar stool?" Small talk was not his forte, but being spoken to by such a beauty did not happen every day. He took a closer look as she began to nurse her Martini; which had appeared from nowhere. He thought he needed to come here more often and immediately felt guilty. Jessica and Casey would not have been pleased. At that moment his cell phone started to buzz.

"Please excuse me, I have to take this call." When Alan called, he answered.

She pouted but nodded fine. He headed for the door as the noise would have been too loud to hear any call. On his way out he looked back to the bar and noticed she had gotten up and was heading towards the Lady's room. On reaching the outside he realized how quiet the rest of the world was in comparison to that bar. Traffic was light and few pedestrians passed by. Duncan scanned the area but saw no threats. Looking south he saw the young lady he sat next to in the bar leaving through a side door. She looked both ways and then crossed the street.

"Well Alan, what's up?"

"Duncan, beyond the chatter about you, the NSA has passed down some overheard conversations that involve you in a very negative way."

"Someone still upset with me?"

'Indeed, they have put a contract out on you, all comers.'

"Alan do we know yet who put out that contract? No, but we do know it was someone here in Washington. They used a burner phone, untraceable. The NSA picked up on your name based on my request for monitoring. What is surprising I it seems the original call came from Frankfurt, Germany."

"Why Germany, anything going on there right now?"

Duncan waited for a response, but it was a long time coming.

"Yes and no. There is a meeting going on right now, all this week, at the Deutsche Bank. It is made up of mostly Arab central banks. It might be worthwhile you going if your contact there is still well connected."

'Alan, Otto Sternberg is still part of the EU Central banking system, so I suspect he will be there for such a meeting."

"Well, there is a Lufthansa flight at 8 pm to Frankfurt. I'll book you on it, Business Class. The ticket will be available for pickup at check-in, but I will email you the itinerary with an open return. Maybe Otto will know something about what is going on."

" While you are at it, have your secretary book me a room at the Park Hotel in Bad Homburg. It is close to Frankfurt just a short train ride, and the best Italian Restaurant in Germany 'Da Alfonso' I can get to the Deutsche Bank easily from the Central Train Station or take the Underground to the Opern Platz, right next door to the bank. I will text Otto and tell him I am coming."

Duncan sent the text suggesting they meet for lunch the next day at the Opern Café. It was already late in Germany, but Otto came back immediately, confirming the meeting and saying he looked forward to seeing Duncan again. Now it was just a waiting game on the plane for the meeting. It was a long nine hours to Frankfurt getting him to FRA at 8 am local time. Passport control was easy, just long lines of tourists and military men returning from leave. The line of non-EU members was always longer and slower than the local lines for EU Passports. A long walk from the gate to passport control and a longer one from there to baggage claim. You walked the length of the airport and then downstair stairs to baggage claim via an escalator. Conveyor belts moved baggage from various parts of the world, all arriving in the early morning. Typical German efficiency, then off to the train station and the central Bahnhof. There was always a short wait for a quick train ride to Bad Homburg from Central. He would retrace these steps to come back to Frankfurt after check-in at the Park Hotel. A casual glance at fellow passengers raised no red flags. A short shower, a change of clothes, would have to do, and then back on the train for the 40-minute ride to the Central Bahnhof. Otto would wait if he was slightly late, but the 13:00-hour meeting should give him enough time.

The ride back to Frankfurt was uneventful. The Central Station was as busy as always. Duncan looked around for anyone taking an interest in him but saw no one. Going outside, he decided against taking the Underground and instead took a taxi from the Bahnhof queue. These taxis would all be the envy of the New York or D.C. ones. All a cream-colored Mercedes Benz. Ten minutes later he was standing in front of the Opern Café. They served the best Oysters in Europe with a cream sauce that made them unforgettable. Looking through the glass entrance door, Duncan could see Otto sitting by the back wall sipping a glass of wine. Undoubtedly a glass of Schloss Vollrads, Riesling, Otto's favorite.

CHAPTER 15

FRANKFURT

"Good Morning, Duncan. Have a good flight over?"

"Quiet and uneventful, which is always welcome."

Duncan ordered the oyster mushrooms and another glass of wine for Otto and himself."

The two continued for another thirty minutes with small talk.

"Here is your pass and lanyard for the meeting tomorrow. This will get you into all venues and the reception and dinner tomorrow evening.' He pushed the pass across the table to Duncan.

"Thanks, Otto. I appreciate it."

" My pleasure, I owed you one for that incident last year in Offenbach. Hopefully, this makes us even?"

Otto smiled as he said this, but there was some truth behind the statement. Duncan had saved his life in a shootout with two terrorists in Offenbach. Both men were in the wrong place at the right time. Duncan again, fired first which gave Otto time to get his gun out and take out the second terrorist.

" You do not owe me anything, but thanks for the pass. I do have a problem, as someone seems to be determined to kill me right now."

"I know, Alan called ahead and brought me up to date on what has been going on. I and my Bank will afford you every courtesy possible while you're here in Frankfurt. You will notice your pass lists you as a representative of the U.S. Central Bank/Federal Reserve. That should not be too far from the truth but, tell me about these attempts on your life and why are you here?"

" NSA picked up some shatter about the attempts on me and they all pointed to Frankfurt. This current meeting here with the EU Central Bank seemed like a good place to start. I am looking into the death of one of our Bankers and Nigel Levick, the director of Security of the Bank of England."

"Any threats here, Duncan?"

" Not that I am aware of, but have you heard anything about either killing among your colleagues at the bank?"

" Yes, something to start with. The rumor mill, one that is very strong among Bankers suggests that both men knew each other well. Apparently, Nigel would alert Haughton if he saw or heard anything that would affect the USA in old Blighty. While this could be considered dirty pool by some, the information flow seemed to go both ways. There is also a South African involved in this information flow. His name is Gert van der Merve. You will meet him tomorrow at the conference. He is the I.T. guy at the REPUBLIC OF SOUTH AFRICAN equivalent of the U.S. federal reserve. Seems like a nice chap, but a little stiff. I have had some dealings with him, but limited. I stumbled on the connection purely by accident some months ago. It appears our Mr Levick enjoyed going to Cape Town, where van der Merve is based. We do try and keep track of where members of various Central banks travel from time to time. Trying to keep ahead of the curve. Think of this as intelligence gathering, keeping surprises down to a minimum. Levick visited CAPE TOWN last June, of course winter there, so he may have just wanted to get away from the heat in London. More than that, I do not know. Van Der Merve does have a bit of a reputation, not always good. Kind of a party animal and known to cut corners, which is why the EU Bank keeps tabs on South Africans. No one has an interest in upsetting any apple carts. Since Apartheid ended everyone is a bit leery of our southern colleagues."

'Thank you, Otto, this has been most helpful. If you could arrange an introduction at the conference tomorrow, I would appreciate it."

'"Will do, but do not underestimate our Mr. Van Der Merve. He has been there for many years and is likely to stay on as perhaps the new managing Director, if I believe everything I hear."

'OK, thanks again, Otto. I will go back to Bad Homburg, get a night's sleep, and be at the conference tomorrow morning at Ten am."

They shook hands and departed. Otto paid for lunch, which would make Alan happy. At least now he had something to report with the new lead to South Africa. Duncan took the underground back to the main Bahnhof and hopped a train to Bad Homburg. One hour later he was back in the hotel and phoning the US with updates. He also called Jessica in her office, but she was too busy to speak with him. Just as well, as he really only wanted to call Casey who was also out of the office. Alan had no new information but found the South African lead interesting. If Casey had anything new, she would have reached out to him via email to call—silence from her end. Otto had been a joy to catch up with, and the pass would be useful for possible future contacts and maybe more on what this was all about. As usual, it was not what you knew, but rather who you knew that carried you forward. Dinner at Da Alfonso would make this part of the trip joyful. He couldn't know if that would carry forward the next day, but why not go to bed after a great meal, a good bottle of Barolo, and a Limoncello as a follow-on? Herr Penna, the owner would never disappoint. They had remained friends long after Duncan returned to the U.S.A. after a ten-year stint in Germany.

The following morning brought typical German weather. This was a country that had dark grey weather from September to May and light grey from June through August. Now once again found him on the train to the main train station in Frankfurt. Then the Underground to the Opera Square area. A short walk to the Deutsche Bank finished this portion of the trip. Security at the Bank was tight, metal detectors, and very large guards with an air of seriousness about them completed the picture. An arrow pointed to the conference area. People were milling about smartly at the top of the escalator. There was a smattering of suits and Arab headdresses among them. Very few women other than uniformed hostesses handing out the day's program on entering the main auditorium area. At first Otto was nowhere to be seen. A tap on his left shoulder alerted him to his friend.

"Good morning! Did you enjoy da Alfonso's last night?"

"I did indeed. Herr Pena remains the Master of his domain."

"Now I see our friend Van Der Merve over there. He is the one with the light grey suit and briefcase.' Let me introduce you."

They walked over to where Van Der Merve was standing. As Duncan and Otto arrived, Van Der Merve turned towards them sensing an approach.

' Good day, Mr. van der Merve. Let me introduce Duncan Innes, who is with the Federal Reserve in Washington."

Both men shook hands. Van der Merve was one of those that never looked anyone in the eyes. A big red flag.

He was a Boer both from name and size. Very large hands and dark eyes. He looked the part of a farmer, not a Banker. He probably came originally from Stellenbosch in the Cape area.

'My pleasure Mr. Innes. please call me Gert. Any friend of Ottos is my friend."

The smile was there, but the eyes were dead.

"By all means, Gert, call me Duncan."

The two men continued chatting in general terms when the gong announced the start of the conference. All three worked their way into the auditorium. Otto moved in another direction leaving Gert and Duncan to find their own seats.

" Duncan, you really must visit us in South Africa."

"To date no particular reason to spend the company's money on such a trip. But otherwise, I would love to."

He smiled as he said it. South Africa was one of his favorite places and in particular Cape Town. Many pleasant evenings were spent in Rondebosch at the Pig and Whistle pub. It had been years since he last visited. Such an invite might be productive.

"Well Duncan, your Bank and mine do have much in common. We both effectively transfer large sums of money through various federal reserves and other institutions around the globe. Lately, there seems to be an increase in traffic from the Middle East."

Duncan knew much of these funds were transferred through South Africa to avoid detection from the US algorithms used to keep an eye on illicit terrorist funds, if at all possible. He had benefited in the past from knowledge gleaned through this source of information via the U.S. Federal Reserve. Now the question was why Van Der Merve offered this information. Although not completely common knowledge, anyone in the U.S. banking sector knew it. Was he being tested?

The lecture on foreign exchange by the speaker droned on and on for another hour. Arcane information at best. It was difficult to stay alert between the talks and jet lag which was catching up. Duncan had learned years earlier that staying under intense light fooled the body into a new time rhythm. While this worked most of the time, speeches such as the current one did not help keep him awake. Gert suddenly stood up and excused himself claiming a need for the men's room.

"See you tonight Duncan? Say goodbye to Otto for me please, I may go to the hotel and then come back."

" I shall look forward to it Gert. Till tonight."

Otto saw Gert leave and nodded to Duncan from across the room.

"Well, did you get what you wanted?"

"Partially, Gert knows something. He invited me to South Africa. He also tried to tell me how his Bank moved money about independent of the U.S.A. knowing anything about it. That was an unsolicited remark. The question is why?"

"Perhaps just showing off. He does strike me as a bit of a braggart."

"Maybe Otto, but there was something else there. I do not ignore gut feelings, and right now, my gut is rumbling that something is not what it appears to be."

The two men shook hands and agreed to meet at the reception that night. Free drinks for Otto, maybe more for Duncan. Duncan also got up and left for his hotel. A shower, a few emails, and a check-in with Alan. Then back for the reception at 19 hours.

He knew he picked up a tail. His neck hairs were on alert. The Deutsche Bank building was solid glass, reflecting everyone within 100 yards of the entrance. Duncan scanned the surrounding area looking for anyone interested in him. On the opposite corner in front of a small garden stood a man with an overcoat busily lighting a cigarette. He was trying very hard to be unnoticeable, but Duncan saw him immediately. He had seen him before in the area of his hotel in Bad Homburg. No coincidence. Duncan started to walk back towards the Opera House and the Metro station that would take him back to the Bahnhof and then Bad Homburg. His newfound shadow kept pace but at a distance. In the center of the Opera Square, Duncan turned east on the Eschenheimer Landstrassse heading towards the Hauptwache. At the entrance to the Metro he took the stairs down to the shopping level and then onto the trains. He occasionally looked back innocently to see if his follower was still with him. Too easy to follow, but then again Duncan did not need to lose him just yet. The train pulled into the station. Duncan got on last. Looking to see where his shadow was and which car he entered. Then they were off to the main station. So far there appeared to be only one follower. At the main Bahnhof, he disembarked, went to track 11 for Bad Homburg and jumped on the new train. No sign now of the shadow who probably just lost interest. That would change later tonight when Duncan went back to the reception. Maybe it was time to have a chat with the shadow. Two emails to Alan with updates on progress and a request for more information on Gert Van Der Merve. No other emails waiting in his inbox, nor messages from anyone. After a late shower and a short pit stop, Duncan put on his evening suit and headed out for his trip back to Frankfurt. The same tail picked him up at the train station. He had no interest in remaining unseen. Duncan nodded to him as he entered the platform. The man followed twenty yards behind. Both men got on the same train leaving the station within five minutes of their arrival. Forty-five minutes later they got off at the Central Bahnhof. The normal crowd of commuters had already thinned. He decided to walk with his tail trailing behind. Up the Kaiserstrasse then over to the Deutsche Bank. The small garden on the right led to the Bank. He wanted to ensure he kept the tail and made him as comfortable with the task as possible. Few pedestrians were going his way. The garden would make the ideal spot for him to take the tail. A lot of trees, dark, and poorly illuminated other than wash from the high rise Banks nearby. Duncan stepped off the sidewalk onto the grass and sat on a convenient park bench. His tail obliged by coming closer. When he was only three feet from Duncan, Th tail realized his mistake in coming that close. Duncan had him around his neck in seconds pulling him into the bushes and behind the trees. No chance anyone saw them. The tail fought back but was no match for the stronger Duncan. The tail was outweighed, too short, and couldn't get enough leverage to break the hold. Both went to the ground. Duncan kept the pressure on him feeling the tails will gradually slipping away. A lack of air does make you slow down.

'Why are you following me, and who sent you?"

The tail did not answer, a consequence of having his windpipe shut. He just shook his head and continued to try and break the hold. Duncan did not want to kill him but did want some answers. He eased up a little on the pressure on the tail's windpipe just enough to cut down on the thrashing about and allow some air into the the lungs.

Duncan reached around to the inner side of the tails coat

and grabbed his wallet. A driver license only produced the name Gunther Mattis and an address in Darmstadt.

'Well Gunther, it would seem we are not making progress. I will ask again, "Who hired you?"

"I was hired to follow you and report on where and to whom you spoke."

'Report to whom?" Duncan increased the pressure again.

"I report to a South African. I do not know his name."

'How do you know he is a South African?"

" I recognized the accent. I had some South African friends that also recommended me for this job."

"You need a better set of friends. These could get you killed or at least seriously injured."

They carried on chatting for a few minutes. Duncan decided to let Gunther go as there appeared nothing more to be gained holding him in the park. As soon as Duncan released the hold, Gunther jumped up and was off and running. All roads seemed to lead to South Africa. With Gert in Cape Town, a trip there was probably a good idea.

The reception was in full swing when Duncan arrived. Otto immediately saw him come in and crossed over to Duncan.

"Are those a few pieces of grass on your suit?"

"I know, I had a tail we had words in the park across from here."

" Is he still alive."

"Yes, he was a Private eye that was hired to keep track of my whereabouts, etc.. That idea was disabused tonight."

"Any idea who hired him and why?"

"None, but he did mention a South African. I would think as Gert knew I was coming here it couldn't be him. What would be the point?"

Duncan gave Otto all of the details of the conversation with

Gunther. The address in Darmstadt was also passed on, but Duncan did not believe it mattered one way or the other.

"So, what do we do next? I do not like my guests in Frankfurt to have these kinds of struggles."

"Right now, I am going to have a few words with Gert and then get back to Alan with the update and me being followed. A trip to RSA seems in order. Any useful contacts down there I can tap into?"

"Yes, I'll text you the contact information. Just be careful, we do not want a repeat of the attempts on your life down there."

At that moment Gert saw them and worked his way over to Otto and Duncan.

"Nice to see you both again." He smiled, but again with the dead eyes. They shook hands all around and caught a passing waiter handing out glasses of wine.

"Cheers!" Otto raised his glass as did Duncan and each took a sip. The wine was horrible. A Riesling but very generic with a tart, and an awful aftertaste. Gert could not help but notice the grass on Duncan's trousers yet chose not to say anything. Maybe he knew already what had happened. Duncan brushed off a few of the pieces. Gert did not seem to notice or be interested.

Gerts next comment cemented the trip to South Africa.

"Duncan, I was informed this afternoon about the attempts on your life. You certainly look none the worse for wear. Any idea who you have annoyed?"

"Not really Gert, but it would appear that some of this has traveled over here. I was being followed from my hotel to here this evening. The tail and I had a few words but he ran off."

'Were you in any danger?"

" I do not think so, but it always pays to be careful. How did you hear about the attacks on my life?"

"It was on my briefing email for this conference this after-noon, the information came from the States. There seems to be a lot of interest in your whereabouts. I had asked who you were in a previous email after we met. " Gert took another sip of the wine and looked at Otto with a 'what is going on look'.

'Well Otto, We can't have our visitors being harassed while here. I will look into the shadow that Duncan picked up, but I doubt much will come from it. Probably just a mugger who thought he had an easy wealthy target."

"Gert, the tail, and I had a short meeting in the park across the street, but he seemed harmless enough. I have passed his contact information on to Otto. Maybe Otto will learn more??? That is why I had some grass pieces on my suit earlier."

"Sounds like you were lucky Duncan. Take care going home, he may have friends." Otto just shrugged. They all broke off the conversation and started to mingle with the other guests. Otto pulled Duncan aside after a half hour of small talk.

"Duncan, I will follow up on the Darmstadt connection, but I doubt you are going to find anything else here tonight or tomorrow."

"I agree, but meeting Gert may have been helpful. Thanks a lot."

'Nothing to thank me for, but if you do meet him in Cape Town, be careful He is well connected down there with many of the dangerous players including the ANC. Those are the polit-ical types and you can be made to disappear.'

"Thanks Otto. I am going to head back to Bad Homburg and call it a night. I'll call you tomorrow before I leave."

The two men shook hands and left the ballroom where the reception had been held. It was now winding down. In another corner of the ballroom, they both saw Gert speaking with an Arab in full mufti.'

Duncan asked " Any idea who he is speaking with now?"

" Yes, that is Omar Assassi a banker from Kuwait. They pass a lot of money through South Africa. We do try and keep an eye on where the funds go, but too many cutouts to be precise."

"Any idea if Gert is into something he shouldn't be?"

'Undoubtedly Duncan, but nothing I can prove. As long as he does not contravene our bank policies or the German Government, we leave him alone. I do know that he has done business with your government from time to time, but not sure what. The CIA has so many different projects running, it is hard to tell who is financing what."

'Well, I will check in with Alan and see what he can find out. If you run into anything, please let me know. Also, please text me the contact you have in Cape Town and perhaps an introduction. Thanks in advance."

'Will do, be careful down there. It is a beautiful country but very dangerous. Avoid Johannesburg, as that is the worst of a bad lot. If you need any other support on your trip, please reach out. I still have some clout in the area."

"Will do, thanks in advance. You be careful too, can't have you injured or worse while I am running about in the lions den"

Duncan left the building and headed back to the Bahnhof for his ride back to Bad Homburg sans tail. There would still be time to stop off at Da Alfonsos for a nightcap; then off to the hotel for emails and phone calls. He needed to check in with Alan, bringing him up to date on Gert's behavior, the tail, and Omar Assassi.

The email to Alan took ten minutes. He asked what the bank knew about Assassi and if anything about Gert van Der Merwe was on file. He also mentioned the potential CIA involvement through funding issues. No answer was expected as it was too late in the evening in Germany and early morning in D.C. It would take a few hours for an answer. Bedtime was at hand with the possibility of sleep an excellent idea. He tried Jessica again, without luck. Casey was also out and about. No news was good news. He knew Jessica was less than pleased right now, but not worth worrying about at least for the present. He left a message on Casey's cell phone and asked her to check in with his flat and see if anything was going on there. Casey had never given his key back, nor had he ever asked for it; prophetic.

When Duncan woke up in the morning four emails were waiting. The first was from Casey. All was well with the apartment and when would he return? The second was from Lt. Fisher who wanted to have another interview and should contact police HQ on his return. The third from Alan described the less-than-savory Assassi. He should call when he could. The last was from Jessica wishing him a good trip and he should call when he got back. As much as he would have liked to avoid a call to Jessica, he knew it couldn't be helped. H decided to call Alan first as that was the most pressing call.

"Good day, Alan. Trust all I well?"

"Not really, I have been inundated with phone calls on your activities and whereabouts.'

"Who is calling?" there was a pregnant pause followed by Alan's response.

"The Vice President's office on multiple occasions. It would appear that you were observed expressing interest in Assasi and Gert. I suspect someone read your email to me asking for more information on both Assasi and Gert.'"

"Why would anyone be interested in those conversations? And, why the V.P.'s office?"

'It turns out, on my other inquiries, that Assasi uses South Africans to transfer money to less than reputable organizations. That doesn't explain why the V.P. is interested unless some national security issue is involved. Let me check with some people over at the NSA and see what they know, if anything. "

'So what should be our next move?" I have no issues with Assasi, however, if there is a connection back to the White house, we probably need to know what it is."

"Agreed", said Alan. "I suggest you get down to Cape Town and see what you can find out. I hate surprises, and after the interest shown in what we are doing by the V.P., it warrants a closer look. Just be careful."

"That is what Otto said. He implied Gert could get me removed rather easily. I'll try and leave no later than tomorrow. See what Assasi is up to if possible. I will check in from Cape Town, probably over the weekend. Otto is lending me one of his contacts. He will be the first stop. Please book me a room at the Adderley Gardens Hotel in the City Center, and the booking should be in two days."

"Will do, but be careful Duncan, I do not want to lose you. We are still trying to find the girl who disappeared in London. No luck so far, though facial recognition did get a possible hit in L.A. That was more about bone structure than an actual direct hit. More when I have it."

"Keep me informed on the search for her and take a look around for any connection to the V.P. Allyson. I still do not know why he is so interested in where we are in this investigation."

Duncan hung up and started to look for possible flights. He would have to fly through Johannesburg and then on to Cape Town. That would make for a long day but do able in business class. He was able to book a Business Class fare for the following evening to Johannesburg with an on-going connection to Cape Town. Getting boarding passes through the Hotel Printer finished off this part of his trip. Yet again a train to the main Bahnhof and another to the airport and his long flight.

After spending time in Johannesburg airport, the first stop, he finally was able to board the Cape Town flight. Once landed it was the hotel by cab and a much-needed recovery night from an otherwise boring trip:

South Africa

CHAPTER 16

CAPE TOWN

The next morning after a full nights sleep, he had a day to kill. He decided to head out to Sea Point and see how the area had changed. From the Point you could see Robbin Island, a prison, which was a throwback to the old Apartheid regime. Now the area was a Mecca for Cafes, Italian restaurants, and tourists from all over the world. The Green Point stadium had been rebuilt and the entire area gentrified. If he had the time he would stop at the Clifton hotel over-looking the ocean and Camps Bay. Another beautiful tourist spot, if still standing. A new sidewalk had been added from Green Point all the way around to Sea Point. It would have been a perfect morning but for the two locals that followed closely behind. One appeared to be playing with a Zulu Assegai, which was a type of short-handled spear. Excellent for close combat but required a lot of practice to be effective. The blade was long with a short handle. Lethal nonetheless. It was starting to look unlikely that he would make the Clifton Hotel. A few joggers were about, but seemingly unaware of the two men and Innes. Duncan slowed allowing the men to catch up and get closer. No time like the present to see what this was all about.

"Boys, what can I do for you?"

Neither man expected to be talking to their victim This was supposed to be an easy job. Take the man out on his walk and make sure he never returns to the city center. Now he was speaking to them. Why? He instead took a step closer. An immediately kicked out with his right foot catching one in the knee. The knee immediately collapsed dropping the victim to the sidewalk. Take a knee out early and most fights are over before they begin. The pain would be impressive and prevent any follow-up retaliation. There was a good chance the assailant would be crippled for life. The other potential attacker had a look of total disbelief as to how quickly his partner had been taken out. He reached into his pants pocket reaching for a short switchblade. Not as impressive as the Assegai, but useful. As his hand came out, Duncan was sending a punch to the man's throat. If you can't breathe, you can't fight. A lesson was learned as the man went down gasping through a broken larynx. Duncan removed the knife from the assailant's hand and turned back to the broken kneecap, who was writhing on the cement sidewalk unable to do anything but groan and whimper. A satisfying outcome for Duncan if not for the kneecap whose leg now had a strong pitch to the side which should have been anatomically impossible.

Duncan stood over the victim placing one foot on the shattered knee.

"Who sent you and why?"

Kneecap shook his head no and continued to try and bend his knee back to its normal position. But the pain was just too much.

"Last chance, or you may not ever walk again."

Duncan continued to apply pressure with his shoe.

"No point looking at your buddy. He is now out of the game. I suspect he will never speak again with a shattered Larynx , but who knows? Your choice if you ever want to walk again. One more time, who hired you and then I will call an ambulance?"

Duncan again applied some pressure to the knee.

Kneecap shrieked and grimaced.

" It was a man by the old Stuttafords Department Store building. A fellow Muslim."

'How do you know that?"

"I have seen him before in the Mosque."

"Not enough lad, I think you will need some more encouragement, which Mosque?"

"JAMIA Majid on the Foreshore." Kneecap went back to moaning and holding his knee.

Duncan promised to call an ambulance for both of them.

At that moment a group of teenagers decided to walk by with a casual glance in Duncan's direction. Time to break the conversation off and move along. He believed the Muslim connection but had little to go on. The next stop looked to be The Jamia Majid Mosque, one of the oldest in the city. There were several Mosques in Cape Town, but Jamia Majid was probably the best known and certainly the oldest. First, he would have to go back to the hotel, check-in, and see if Otto had come through with a local contact or anything new from Alan McDonald. There were indeed three emails again. The first from Alan said, please call immediately on receipt of this email. The second was from Jessica again asking when he would come back and lastly from Casey also asking for a call. With a seven-hour time difference, it seemed a little rude to call Alan McDonald at four am.

"Good morning Alan, you did say call right away."

"I Know. We have some news and do you have anything to share?"

"Indeed I do. Another attempt on my life today. Two Muslims in Cape Town tried to get me on my walk near Sea Point."

"I am not surprised. My news meets with yours in that the NSA passed on some notes to me. They think someone in Iran is highly interested in your activities. Lots of calls back and forth to South Africa and a series of questions on whether you have met up with Gert van der Merwe as yet and who did Otto send to you"

"So far I have not heard from Otto, very unusual, but the two Muslims were told to get me by some other Muslim, or so they thought."

"Where are the two attackers now?"

"I suspect they are in the hospital, I called an ambulance for them. One has a severely damage larynx and the other a shattered kneecap. They are no longer in the game."

"What's your next move other than staying alive?"

'I am going to call Otto next, and then off to the main Mosque for a while. May not be worth the time, but my presence should create a bit of a stir for someone. Hopefully, Otto can help with his contact. Otherwise, I am dead in the water."

"Okay, stay safe and keep reporting in as you can. There is a Muslim connection. As you know the V.P. has been tasked to look after what is going on in Iran. Now the buzz around here is the 'Shia Crescent of Power as the latest phrase of interest. It would appear that Iran, Iraq, and Syria are all under one umbrella, funded by Iran. Iran needs access to the Mediterranean. We know they want to build a pipeline over Syria for Med access. That would pressure the Saudis, the UAE and Kuwait. Iran could cut off ocean access easily through the Straits of Hormuz. A catastrophe for the world economy, but good for Iran and indirectly Russia. Obviously not in our best interests."

"Why come after us, personally?"

"We are getting too close to something going on. My question is it the Iranians, the Saudis or someone else?"

'If we are getting close, I need a scorecard or a program. I have no idea what is going on."

"For my money, I would guess the Iranians are behind all of this. Still checking with the Saudis as they have an interest in this game."

Duncan paused to think about that and then said, 'What interest do the Sauds have?"

"Short answer is their number one enemy for the hearts and minds of the Arab world are the Iranians. Imagine a scenario where the Iranians close off the gulf to all oil tankers from Kuwait, the U.A.E and Iraq. The world market chaos would benefit Iran and bring Western economies to a standstill and hurt Saudi Arabia's revenue stream. If Iran can build the pipeline through Iraq and Syria to the Med, they would effectively control the West's economies. Their income from oil exports to the West and Europe would be astronomical. The Russians would be thrilled as their prices for energy would vastly increase. Saudi Arabia would be more or less dead in the water. We could not make up for that loss of energy with our exports. That makes the Saudis by default an interested party to what Iran does. How do we react as a country? This all refers back to the Shia Crescent of Power we discussed. There are billions of dollars at risk here for the Europeans, the USA and Russia. Russia would love this scenario. Some in our country would also like it, but it would be short lived."

'Sorry Alan, how does this make you and I involved?"

"I do not know for sure, but someone is being paid off to

insure we do not find out what is behind all of this. As two bankers are dead, a number of attempts on us, why?"

There was silence on the phone for two minutes while both thought about what they knew at this point. Neither wanted to break the other's train of thought.

"Give Otto a call and get back to me with what you find out. I am going back to bed for at least two hours. Good luck."

Duncan replied, "I'll call Otto and get the connection there. I will call you back. In the meanwhile, see if you find any traces of payments via South Africa to anyone in D.C. area. Email me if you get anything. Also please call Lt. Fischer and tell him I am out of the country and can't call him back. See if you can get him to quit on me as a person of interest. He is trying to set up another interview. I will let you know what Otto says."

Duncan chose to call Otto first, however, he was not available. The secretary said he would call back in thirty minutes or email. With a wait time of thirty minutes Duncan decided to call Casey first. It was still early, but she was an early riser, so he could catch her at home.

"Good morning Casey. Time to rise and shine."

Chapter 17

The Cape

"Duncan it is 5;30 in the morning. I am up but not happy about that. What is going on?"

"Someone tried again to get rid of me. It appears this is becoming a habit."

"Are you all right? No injuries and what does the other guy look like?"

"Broken knee cap otherwise hail and hearty. He will not forget me anytime soon. And speaking of forgetting, thanks for looking in at my apartment. And, I have not forgotten you. I owe you big time. As soon as I get back, let's do dinner again without the interruptions."

"I would love that, assuming you get back in one piece."

"I'll be back, just do not know when. Still busy here." A that moment the hotel phone began to chime.

Duncan hung up and answered the hotel phone.

"Hello?"

"Hello, Mr. Innes. My name is Marlee Johansen. Otto Sternberg asked me to contact you."

'Oh, Hi, Marlee yes indeed. When can we meet? I can come to you or any suggestions are welcome."

"Certainly, how about this afternoon at Paola's in Sea Point at one pm? I have a green dress on now, and a black purse, blond hair, and five feet 7 inches tall. That makes me a little taller than most girls here. Does that work for you?"

"The height or time" Duncan laughed as he said it.

"The time of course."

"Okay great see you then. Lunch sounds good, or just coffee?"

"Lunch would be grand. Till one then, enjoy the morning."

Duncan hung up and emailed Alan with this latest update. He tried again to call Jessica, but she was out of the office.

Of course the question was what did Marlee do for the bank if anything. At least he now had a contact and things were starting to look up. A quick email and a prompt response from Otto confirmed Marlee was the contact and wished him luck. Now to kill some time until lunch. Walking along the Sea Point shore did not seem like a good idea in light of recent experiences. He chose to wander about downtown Cape Town along the Foreshore area, another section rebuilt since his last trip and offering easy walking access to the Port and Cruise ships he could see moored there. He was careful to look for anyone taking an interest in him, but no one was evident. Since the Foreshore was close to the Mosque, he took a short stroll towards it, looking at everyone passing by. A few young men seemed to be heading in the general direction, but they displayed no interest. The building had seen better days, but so had the two assailants who accosted him in Sea Point. There appeared little to be gained from hanging around. Duncan stopped at a small café and ordered a cup of coffee and a croissant. The coffee was good and strong. The croissant was a little on the stale side but would do until lunch. Another hour and he would meet up with Marlee. A cab seemed like a good idea and many were readily available. The Foreshore was a busy place for cabs and they cruised in packs like wolves looking for passengers or lunch. One picked him up and started to drive towards Sea Point. A short ride of maybe ten minutes. He got out of the taxi twenty feet from the entrance to Paolas. Small crowd already seated.

"Table for two please. Near the front if possible."

"Follow me Sir. Anyone else joining you?"

"Since I requested a table for two, I would have thought the answer to that question obvious?"

A quick yes sir, and he was led to a small table overlooking the Ocean and in the distance Robbin Island. The entrance was open and allowed a view of anyone coming in or leaving. Marlee was right, she was taller than anyone else of the ladies already in the restaurant. What she failed to mention was how beautiful she was. This was not someone you met in the hopes no one saw you or remembered you. All eyes were on her as she walked towards Duncan's table.

"Otto had described you Mr. Innes, so easy to spot."

"Otto did not describe you or I would have reached out to you yesterday. You're not just tall, but quite stunning as well."

"Well thank you, kind sir. Now that we have all the pleasantries out of the way, Otto said you were looking for some information from the Bank. If possible, I should help you. As Otto is a good friend and has helped me in the past, I am happy to help you as his friend, but confidentially."

"Can we start with a short description of what you do for the Bank?"

"Certainly, I am in charge of all handling of money transfers both inbound and outbound, along with a small staff. You do understand that anything I say to you is confidential as I could lose my job if anyone found out I spoke to you."

"Understood, I will keep your name and information to myself."

"What exactly are you looking for?" She looked quizzically at Duncan.

"I am looking for any incoming transfers from Kuwait in the past twelve months and where the transfers went if possible after you received it."

"I know that one off the top of my head. Last January there were two transfers from Kuwait. One for twenty five million U.S. Dollars and another three days later for thirty million. Both went immediately out to the Bank of England. It's the sum that made me remember it. Normally we only get transfers for about one million from Kuwait maximum. These two were very unusual and were personally handled by our Department of Security Head, Gert Van Der Merve. He would rarely be involved, and if, then only with the Chairman's approval. I received copies of the transfers for the files, but that is all."

"Do you know who at the Bank of England the transfers were directed towards?"

" Yes, the correspondent was Nigel Levick. I believe he is Security at the Bank of England as well."

"Thank you very much, Marlee. This has been helpful. They always say follow the money."

"That is really all I know about the transfers. I hope this information has been of help?"

"It has indeed, I will tell Otto you were a gem. Thank you for your assistance. Do not tell anyone that you spoke with me or what we discussed. I will do the same for you. I am sure that Otto will help you in the future in any way he can."

" I certainly will not say anything to anyone, and thank you for lunch. I have to get back to the Bank." Marlee stood, offered a hand and started to leave. Duncan would miss her. Great accent, great legs, and a real beauty. Sometimes lunch was worth the cost. The information put him further in Otto's debt. The start of a trail. All transfers in late January and early February. Now he had to track the money. The S.W.F.T. system could be avoided as it was Intrabank. Alan was going to have to start pulling in favors from the Brits. The email to Alan described the conversation and the sums transferred and to whom. Alan would have his work cut out for him tracking that information down. Duncan looked at Marlee's business card again. Phone number, and office address all on it. It was an easy decision to call her office and see if she was available for dinner that evening.

"Hi Marlee, I wondered if you were available for dinner tonight? Perhaps the Mount Nelson at 8 pm?"

"It took a minute for a response, but he could hear her breathing and other office noises in the background.

"Sure, if asked I will say that our mutual friend Otto arranged a dinner date for one of his friends. Does that work for you?" She seemed to be smiling as she said this.

"Yes, good idea. You might mention this to a few people in the office in case we are seen together, innocent enough."

He looked forward to seeing her again but felt guilty about Jessica and Casey. If anyone did see them together it would look innocent enough. Otto was known to Gert van Der Merve, and it made sense he would arrange such a meeting for his friend. In the meantime, he would call Gert and set up another meeting in the City. That took only five minutes and it was agreed to meet outside of Cape Town in Rondebosch the following morning for lunch. Again he checked emails to see if anything new was afoot. Absolute dead silence. As it was late afternoon in Cape Town a call to Alan seemed in order. With a seven-hour time difference, Alan would be in his office as this was a normal work day. His secretary, Mary, picked up the call and said Alan was in a meeting with someone she did not know.

'Any idea when he will be free?'

"Sorry no. When I came in this morning his door was already shut and I could their voices. Should I interrupt him on the intercom and let him know you're on the line?"

"No thanks, just tell him I called and I can be reached for the next hour or so and then offline. Thank you, Mary."

"Will do, safe travels."

Duncan opted for a quick shower and a change of clothes. Marlee would be dressed to the nines for dinner at the Mount Nelson, the posh hotel in Cape Town. The grounds around the hotel were beautiful. Basically a full botanical garden with a heavy emphasis on proteas and some exotic flowers. He found himself looking forward to seeing her again. This time, a dinner just for fun, no work.

Duncan got to the Mount Nelson at 7;30 pm. There were a number of guests milling about and some walking in the Gardens. He chose to sit in the lobby bar and watch the door for Marlee. He was not disappointed. She came through the large entrance hall causing quite a stir. There are truly very few beautiful people you can run into day to day, Marlee however was one of them. She wore a red knee length dress with sash. Her hair was swept up in the back and sides. She would take any man's breath away and did as she walked through the lobby towards the bar. She waved a small acknowledgment that she had seen him and was coming over. The bartender was immediately attentive.

" A martini please with an olive."

"Yes ma'am, coming right up."

"Well, Marlee, you are certainly stunning tonight. I enjoyed watching the guests observe your walk through the lobby."

'Thank you Duncan. I appreciate the invite. It has been some time since I last came here. By the way, I did as you suggested and let it be known I was having a dinner date with a friend of a German acquaintance. The only one interested was Gert Van Der Merve. He asked to be remembered, which I promised to do. He knew you were in town but did ask how I knew you. I told him you were a friend of Otto's whom I had met at a conference in Germany two years ago. I was having dinner with you as a favor to Otto.

"How did he respond to that piece of information?"

"Surprisingly well. He said he knew you and understood why Otto made the introduction."

'I will have to thank Otto for that. I do enjoy seeing you. Let's go in and get some dinner as promised."

"I'd love to, they have a Beef Wellington that is supurb."

"I do love a carnivore. Somewhat rare in young ladies today. A salad just doesn't say dinner, besides which, salad is what my dinner eats."

They dined as promised and the food was excellent. Service was also good, and the setting was reminiscent of colonial times. Probably politically incorrect but great fun. When the check arrived, Duncan pulled out his wallet and placed a credit card on the silver tray. Marlee just smiled and took a last sip from her second glass of wine.

"As they walked outside through the gardens, Duncan asked, " May I call you a taxi to take you home?"

"I rather thought you could ride home with me for a coffee and or nightcap. I live in Disa Park on the side of Table Mountain very close by here. It is one of the silo- looking buildings you can see from anywhere in the city. The view is spectacular and I thought you might enjoy something other than a hotel this evening?"

"Yes indeed, sounds great. I appreciate the offer and I promise to behave like a gentleman."

'Well, I certainly hope not or I wouldn't have invited you back to my place" she said with a large grin on her face.

"Sounds good to me, let's find a taxi, and home it is."

"Twenty minutes later and they were entering her building. A lift to the eighth floor took them to her flat. The view was indeed fantastic. The room shape was odd in that it was a circular building. Large picture windows with a narrow entrance way. The furniture was nice if understated. Few pictures on the wall to detract from the beautiful view of the City and the Port. Lights everywhere in the distance. The occasional flashing blue lights of a black Mariah cruising on patrol. Very quiet for being in the city. Sound didn't carry up to the flat.

"At the risk of being a cliché, let me change, and there is a bottle of Sauvignon Blanc in the fridge. Bottle opener in the first drawer to the right of the fridge. Please pour us one and I will be right back. Glasses over the counter on the rack."

"Happy to oblige. I will try and remain patient if possible in your presence."

She let out a small laugh and disappeared into what he believed was the bed room. Two glasses, quick dust off and then opening the bottle. Nicely chilled, a wine from the Stellenbosch region. Duncan sat on the sofa overlooking the city and enjoyed the view. In the far distance Blouberg Strand. A golf course off to the right in the distance and DeWaal drive directly below. This would be an expensive flat for anyone.

When Marlee returned in a silk dragon kimono robe, Duncan smiled and let out a large breath of air.

"Thank you again, that was a nice compliment. "I will join you and have a sip of that wine. Do you like the view?"

"Magnificent. How do you afford this? The bank can't pay that well."

"My parents were quite well off. I grew up in Paarl, over there to the right under that mountain range. They owned a large winery, a bottle of which you are now enjoying. They left me rather well off, so I can indulge in this one sin. It was through them that I got the job at the bank. Their connections ran deep in the politics of the Cape. I needed to do something and majored in B. Comm at the University of Cape Town so the Bank was a logical stop."

They both sipped the wine and looked out over the City.

"Really very beautiful Marlee, both the view and of course you. This kimono is really something." When she leaned forward for her wine glass, the left lapel drifted open revealing a perfectly formed breast seemingly yearning to be free. Duncan reached over and gently pulled her over to his side. His lips sought out hers and she helped leaning into him. There was no doubt an attraction existed between the two of them. Each felt it and the heat they generated seemed to warm the entire room. Marlee stood up and extended an inviting hand. They made their way into the bedroom, where she dropped her kimono onto the small Ottoman at the end of the bed. Duncan reached out to her waist and pulled her closer. She began to pull his shirt off running her nails from his neck downwards. They both laughed. This was turning out to be a great evening and Otto was going to be owed big time. They spent the next two hours in various embraces and when over both were spent. Light was beginning to peek through the mountains to the northeast heralding the arrival of morning. She looked magnificent laying peacefully in her bed, hair splayed on the pillow. This one would be hard to leave, but he must for the lunch with Gert Van Der Merve. A short cab ride to the hotel, shower and change of clothes, check emails, and make a few calls. Back to the job.

CHAPTER 18

RONDEBOSCH

atching a cab turned out to be very easy. There was a small taxi stand outside of Disa Park, ostensibly for residents. A few minutes later he was in the hotel. Reception had a note from Gert Van Der Merve reminding him of lunch. There were also two calls: one was from Otto and the other Alan and both required a callback.

"Good day Otto, how are things in the land of grey?"

"Fine Duncan. I did follow up on your assailant, he was telling the truth. He has no connections to us or your bank. He was merely paid to keep an eye on you. My friends in the Darmstadt police put the fear of God into him. Nothing more there to report. What about you, anything new in Cape Town?"

"Well, yes and no. I am having lunch with Gert today. I had dinner with Marlee last night. I owe you a big thank you, she is lovely. I also know that money was transferred to the Bank of England through South Africa. Twenty-five and thirty million to be exact. Where the transfers went from there is anyone's guess, that I think is the Levick connection. Now I am looking for the Haughton involvement. I suspect he was in contact with Levick and was told something he was not supposed to know. It does not as yet appear to be terrorist-related. I'll know more when Alan follows up. In any case thank you for Marlee and Gert. Marlee is quite a find for anyone. I will let you know what I find. In the meanwhile, if you have any contacts in London, see if you can get information on the two wire transfers."

"Any idea of the time period?"

"My guess would be about late January or early February last year. Both transfers would have made the Bank in late January, but I doubt they would have stayed long. Must have gone towards the USA if Haughton at the Fed was involved?"

'I'll get on it right away. Stay safe. Remember Gert is dangerous and has dangerous friends."

"Thanks, Otto, I will call you in a few days, or leave me another message to call." They hung up. Duncan was thinking about Marlee when the hotel phone rang."

"You just slipped out of the apartment without a thank you ma'am?" She sounded a little piqued.

"Sorry, Marlee, I had to get back to my hotel, change make a few calls, and get ready for lunch with Gert in Rondebosch. I had a great evening, and certainly can't remember spending a greater time with anyone."

"Well that mitigates your behavior somewhat, but I normally do not do one-night stands. Want to come over this evening for a home-cooked meal?"

"Certainly, what time should I arrive and what can I bring?"

"How about 7:30 and bringing a bottle of KWV Brandy would be nice."

"I will be there. Do you mean you can cook as well?"

"I can indeed. It will be fish tonight."

"You are looking better and better and closer to perfect, which for me is a shock and frankly scary. I eat a lot of T.V.

dinners at home. See you tonight." She laughed again and hung up.

It was now however time to get to Gert in Rondebosch. He would also need to find a package store for the KWV. The taxi took forty-five minutes with all of the traffic on Main Road. Getting through Mowbray and the hospital traffic was the hardest, but once in Rosebank, everything quieted down. When they arrived at the restaurant, there were just a few people outside. Gert was already inside and could be seen through the picture window. He was sipping a glass of Red as Duncan came through the main entrance.

"Good morning, Duncan, glad you took me up on my offer to visit Cape Town. Please have a seat. This is a great Red if you would like a glass?"

"Thank you, Gert, I would like it very much."

"Did you enjoy your dinner with Marlee?"

'I did indeed. She was lovely. I will have to thank Otto for that introduction. We had a wonderful dinner at the Mount Nelson."

"Glad to hear it. What finally brought you down here to South Africa? When we spoke you were unsure whether you would come."

"Last minute arrangement. The Bank asked me to drop a package off in Johannesburg on arrival here that was somewhat sensitive for one of the depositor clients. I managed that and then thought why not catch up with one of Otto's friends while here? Cape Town has always been one of my favorite cities in the world. What's not to love?"

"I also decided to take a few vacation days and enjoy the Cape. Probably head over to Camps Bay tomorrow for a swim and look around. I remember the area as spectacular, to say the least." Gert then said,

"If there is anything I can do for you Duncan to make your

trip better, just let me know and there is something I would like to ask if possible?"

"Do you know what happened to Mr. Haughton at the Federal Reserve? I had heard that he was murdered."

"He was indeed, it is still being investigated. So far no leads." Gert still didn't look Duncan in the eye.

" What about the attempts on you? As I said in Frankfurt you had made our internal news as a target?"

"For some unknown reason, I have been targeted, and here I thought I spread sweetness and light everywhere I go."

"Any chance you were set up to be mugged. A simple robbery?"

"No, it has happened several times. So far, I have been lucky."

"Let's hope it stays that way. This place is known for its Greek food, so what would you like?" Duncan glanced again at the menu and opted for the Lamb Kebabs. Gert chose the safe Greek salad. As Gert ordered, Duncan casually looked outside to the street but saw nothing alarming. The waiter took Duncan's order and left. Duncan had seen that across the street there was a package store where he could pick up the KWV Brandy that Marlee requested.

"Duncan, how long are you going to be in Cape Town? I ask, as possibly you might like to visit my vacation house this weekend in Knysa on the beach as my guest. Can't hurt to have closer ties to your Bank.Ż

"I will be here another week and then back to D.C.. A visit to Knysa sounds great, thank you."

"Fine, I'll pick you up at your hotel tomorrow at 10 am if that is OK with you? It takes a few hours to get there. We will come back on Sunday evening. You should enjoy the trip. Knysa has elephants which are unusual for this part of South Africa.

We also have our complement of baboons and other indigenous animals. Beautiful beaches should be fun for you."

"Sounds great, thanks, Gert. Z

" Anything I can bring for you? Wine, Whiskey, or whatever?"

"No Duncan, just some comfortable clothes it will be warm. Walking shoes if you have them or trainers. I believe you call them sneakers will do fine."

"Will do. I always have my running shoes or sneakers. But right now, I am late. Thank you for a fine lunch and the invitation. I shall look forward to it. I am staying at the Adderley Gardens hotel by the way."

"Duncan, I know which hotel. Marlee told me this morning. She did say she had a wonderful evening. I am jealous, but of course, it is taboo to date office staff."

"The same in the USA. Such dating is frowned upon by most H.R. departments. Sets a bad example to others in the company. Again, thank you, I'll look forward to tomorrow. Right now I plan on a bit of shopping in this little town of Rondebosch." Duncan got up, shook hands, and headed for the door. Once outside, he crossed the street towards the package store. Looking back he saw Gert leaving the restaurant and getting into his car. The car pulled into traffic and left. Duncan went into the store and started to look for the KWV bottles.

The ride in the lift up to the 7th floor went smoothly. No other passengers, although the building was fully rented. He found himself looking forward to seeing Marlee again. She did not disappoint. When the door to her flat opened she stood in the frame wearing a black jumpsuit. The color set off her blonde hair nicely and of course her spectacular figure added to the overall allure. The large welcoming grin also warmed him nicely.

"Glad to see you again Marlee."

"Please, come in. I'll take that bottle if I may. By the way, I am impressed you found it. It is a rarity in Cape Town. KWV has won many international competitions and is usually exported. I am sure you will like it. My father swore it was the best brandy in the world. Of course, he was biased towards South African productions.

'We are having a Galijon fish for dinner. A friend had caught this one and I froze it for a few days. These fish make an excellent grilled fish usually cooked outdoors. I am sure you will like it. Like the Springbok, a symbol of South Africa, the Galijoen is our national fish. Looks a little funny, but tastes great. Takes its name from old galleon ships of yesteryear that plied our waters. As a child, we would make these fish at a Braavleis or barbeque. You cannot fish them commercially but they can be caught by private fishermen and brought home, they remain protected.

"Sounds good, and certainly smells good. Anything I can do to help while you finish up in the kitchen?"

"Open that bottle of wine on the counter, pour two glasses and we will be good to have dinner."

"My pleasure." He found himself staring at her again. A lovely sight as she worked in the kitchen plating dinner. This could easily become a habit. Dinner and desire could easily be called a life necessity. Patience was required, if not easily delivered. She motioned him to the table and brought two plates out of the kitchen with her.

The dinner was indeed delicious. The fish was melt-in-yourmouth tender and did not have a fishy taste. A little bit of lemon squeezed on top brought out the flavor. Marlee could cook. She had made a melee of vegetables that steamed in front of him. They were also good, not overcooked as so many vegetables were. They still had a bit of crunch and complimented the fish nicely.

"My compliments to the Chef. Outstanding dinner and certainly one that will be remembered." She smiled at him as he lauded her cooking skills. I certainly could get used to this he thought, while realizing that would be impossible. Duncan was not about to move to South Africa, and he doubted Marlee would leave. The roots were too deep. It was a surprise to realize that he even thought of this as a remote possibility. Marlee was indeed a keeper for most men. But, most men did not have his type of job.

"You have gone quiet Duncan. Anything wrong?"

"Not at all. I was thinking how wonderful it is here with you and how much I enjoyed looking at you and your company."

"Well, now that we have finished up dinner, let's repair to the sofa, enjoy the view and each other. Coffee coming right up."

Duncan helped clear the table, bringing plates to the kitchen. Marlee was cleaning the debris into the waste bin and placing plates in the dishwasher. The coffee machine was doing its thing and gurgling away. Two cups were placed next to the pot. Duncan filled each cup adding a little milk to hers as he had seen at the Mount Nelson. He carried them both to the sofa placing them on the end tables. The view was still stunning. A well-lit cruise ship was being escorted into the harbor by two tugs. Marlee came back into the living room and sat next to him. He could hear the dishwasher begin its cycle behind them. She snuggled up against his side and also looked out over the bay.

"I could get used to this, but I know you will leaving soon."

'Yes, probably in a week but I have to go tomorrow to Gert's summer home in Knysa." My bank thinks it is a good idea to further cement relations with your bank. We have held a bit of distance from your Bank and yet have a close relationship with the European version of our Fed.

"Will this bring you to South Africa more often?"

"I would love that if it meant I could see you, but not sure. My role is not really as a banker, but rather an investigator and or fixer if there is a problem on our end. I haven't had a call to come here in the past five years. But certainly with you here there is a strong reason to come back as often as I can."

" I would like that Duncan. This relationship seems too short and right now, instead of talking about leaving, let's go back to the bedroom. I want you now."

"Yes ma'am, I am ready. Coffee done, everything cleaned up, need to make a mess of another room."

The next morning was a repeat of the previous one. Duncan left early to get to his hotel for the 10 a.m. pickup by Gert. Still, some emails and phone calls to make before the trip. A quick change of clothes, pack lightly, and arrange for the hotel to hold his stuff and be available when he returned Sunday evening. Alan had sent an email overnight which awaited Duncan when he fired up his laptop. Casey had also said hello by email, now he felt guilty.

"Hi Alan, sorry to be calling again so late in the night for you. It is early morning here. Anything new on your end?"

"Call anytime, just bring me up to date. So far nothing new on our mystery girl. If she is out there she will turn up on our radar. We had a possible hit a few days ago, but couldn't be sure."

"Not a lot to report on this end. I did make contact with a bank employee and she was helpful. I have already told you about the transfers from Kuwait and to London which came from her. Anything new on what happened to them?"

'Yes, we know they were broken up into tranches and forwarded to The Caymans and the Bahamas. Working on the recipients now. NSA has gotten quite good at that, anti-money laundering and all that. I should have more later today. What about you, any more attempts to kill you? Or are you making friends?"

'No, lucky so far. I am being picked up this morning by Gert for a trip to his summer home in Knysa. It's about a five hour drive from here, but it will give me a chance to speak with him at length."

Chapter 19

Knysa

"What is the play with him?"

"I think there may be an opportunity to turn him into a source for us on transactions through his Bank to organizations we may have an interest in, but just a thought now."

"Good luck, that would be a great idea if you can get him to join us indirectly. Any idea of the cost involved?"

"Not yet, but having someone inside here would be a positive move on our part. More after the weekend with him." "Be careful with the money transfers, I suspect they may be dangerous. They have tried to kill us both just on a suspicion we may know something. I would think they would try harder if we knew, where the money went and what this is all about." Duncan hung up and grabbed his overnight bag for the Knysa trip. A quick call to Marlee, again thanking her for a wonderful dinner and he would be back on Sunday evening. Perhaps dinner again? They agreed on an eight pm time and would leave what she cooked up to her. She sounded happy to hear from him and wished him a good ride. Over dinner last night they had briefly chatted about Gert's trip and how beautiful Knysa was. The last call to make was to Casey. He tried to reach her at the Precinct but she was unavailable. Seemed to be the current state of affairs.

Outside, Gert was waiting in his car ready to leave. The engine was idling as Duncan approached. Gert jumped out of the car.

"Good morning, all set to go?"

"Yes Gert, will just throw my bag in the back seat and we can leave. I understand this is a long drive?"

"About 5 hours on the Garden route. It is really quite beautiful. You will see a lot of animals and few people. Our first stop will be for a late lunch in Mossel Bay and then on to Knysa. I always enjoy the drive and am sure you will as well. Do you have everything?"

"Yes, I am good to go. Traffic seems rather light for a Friday in the City."

"It is because Monday is a national holiday so many people take Friday off as well to make a long weekend. Today is a good day to travel in South Africa."

They started to drive out of the city making small talk about the weather, the drive, and health. Gert asked about the upcoming general elections in the USA and expressed his opinions on the running candidates; none of which were positive. Duncan chose to ignore his remarks on The U.S.A. As they approached Mossel Bay the scenery changed somewhat. The high desert was behind them. Now everything was much greener. They did pass a troop of baboons feeding on the side of a hill.

'One has to be careful of those animals, they will throw stones at cars and generally make a nuisance of themselves. A few cars were parked on the side of the road looking at the baboons. One larger animal sat on the bonnet of a car and stared at the driver and passengers. You could easily get the feeling, the animal wanted to drive away with the car. The intelligence was evident in the animals eyes, but feral none the less. Gert kept driving into the town only stopping at a small café for lunch.

"I have stopped here for years whenever I drive to Knysa. I also always buy their Biltong for home. Very similar to the American Pemican. Chewy, but tasty. You should try some. It's a meat dried in the sun made from Springbok."

"Thanks I will try a piece after lunch. Just a sandwich or similar will work for me if possible."

" I asked you to come along on this trip as I thought we may be able to forge some closer ties with your fed and mine."

"Sounds good to me, but there are some concerns about your recent activities transferring money for whom we believe to be terrorist organizations."

" As you know we do not keep track of such organizations as your country does. When we transfer funds, it is normally on behalf of another country. We do a lot with the Middle East. But, you know that. I am sure on occasion we have affected transfers that are questionable, but never deliberate. That would go against Bank policy."

" I am sure that has never been your intention. What we would be looking for is a heads-up when questionable transfers are routed through you. Specifically where and to whom. "

"You do realize that what you are asking would go against bank policy and could get me fired. Besides, how would I decide which transfers are legit and which are not?"

"Tell me about some of your clients now of course confidentially."

"We do work with Kuwait, the U.A.E. and Saudi Arabia. With the new shuffling of power in the Middle East we are trying to maintain a neutral stance."

"Describe the shuffling please, so I can understand your perspective."

"Saudi Arabia finds itself along with the other two countries I mentioned in a difficult spot. Iran is flexing its muscles and expanding its influence in Iraq, Syria, and Lebanon. The Saudis are afraid that if Iran gets much bolder they will have to get into a shooting war. Iran wants to build a pipeline through Iraq and Syria to gain access to the Mediterranean. This would allow them access to major markets they could take away from the Saudis. It does not take a wild imagination to picture Iran closing the straits preventing Kuwait and Gulf states from exporting their oil. The result would be higher per barrel oil prices which would benefit Iran and Russia as an added plus. This would lead to chaos in the energy market and allow Iran a short-term corner on the oil market. It has been described as the Shia Crescent of Power and with hatred of the Shia by the Sunnis in the South grounds for war become very real. That is the real impetus of all that is going on in the Middle East. Israel is just a short-term apparition a diversion if you will. Keeps the Americans and the Europeans focused away from Iran on to Israel. This conflict with Hamas keeps the world's attention on Israel. We naturally want no part of these geopolitical machinations. But, I assume you know all of this. Terrorists are a short-term problem and a distraction. "

Our only concern now is to stay on the right side of the law. Whether the Arabs decide to kill one another or not is of little concern. Why are you so interested in our transfers?"

' We think, something more sinister is going on in the Mid-East. Chatter from Iran suggests they are planning something very big and we do not as Americans or the Bank wish to be caught flat footed. It has been my experience that if you follow the money, you will get answers as to what is going on."

"Indeed Duncan, however that is a little beyond what you do for the bank isn't it?"

"Yes it is, however, someone keeps trying to kill me as I run down this rabbit hole. I would rather like that to stop."

"Well, what do you want from me?"

"I would like a periodic update on large sums of money being transferred from the Mid-East through you and where they go."

"That will be very hard to do as it is too general. If you have something specific in mind I will consider it, however it will be expensive."

"Money is not a problem, however, I am sure we can make arrangements that will satisfy you."

" I keep an account in Nassau which would do nicely. Can we say, $10,000 per month for starters?"

" I will have to get back to you on that. Text me your Bank details. As a sign of good faith, please get me a copy of all trans-fers from the Middle East in the last year through your Bank and where they went. I am looking for origin, sums, dates, and destinations. This first tranche will initiate any payments to you going forward. Does that work for you? Get me your banking information in Nassau and I will get the ball rolling based on your first data dump to me as requested. If this works, I shall look forward to a long profitable relationship and you will have a friend at the U.S. Fed. I will be your only contact, which should make security easier for both of us. "

"Great, now let's enjoy Knysa our style. Your room is at the top of the stairs, first door to the right. We will have a cookout or Braavleis at 8 pm. Come back down whenever you're ready and we can enjoy a glass of wine before dinner. Tomorrow I will show you the best beach in South Africa."

"Very well, I will just take a shower and come down. It was a long drive. See you shortly."

the far 'left' and the I don't give a damn middle. If you turn the T.V. on, assuming you have the stomach for it, you will be met by the flavor of the day and the bias of that Station. Now we tend towards more and more Barbies as news readers. Some can't read, but pretend well. Eye candy at best."

" Can't say we are much better here in South Africa. The SABC, our government-owned T.V. service, has its own agenda and pursues it with vigor."

"Most of our TV in the USA is privately owned. Now the so-called cable services are taking a bigger chunk of the viewing public. In the end effect, you get to pay for the bias and propaganda now that once was free."

"By the way, on what we discussed coming over here, I shall be leaving Cape Town for London on Friday, so if you could get me the information before I leave, I will take care of the rest."

"What's in London?"

" I will be visiting an old friend and meeting up with Otto again as he will be there for that weekend. A small meeting with the Bank of England has been called by the EU Bank in Frankfurt. Otto drew the short straw."

"So you are leaving on Friday?"

"Yes, KLM to Heathrow. A 12 hour flight plus one stop. I will get there mid day on Saturday. A long trip indeed."

CHAPTER 20

CAPE TOWN

"Well, we can catch up on Thursday afternoon. I suggest your hotel if that works for you? Say, around three pm?"

"Good, that will work."

"Now, I think Samuel is ready so we should enjoy our dinner."

They did enjoy their dinner and continued to discuss South African and American politics throughout. Early bedtime followed by yet another meal, breakfast, and then off to the beaches. Everything that could be discussed openly was and the rest small talk. Duncan tried Casey again that evening to no avail. The next day was the long haul back to Cape Town. Both men were careful to not bring up the coming information exchange. Duncan did enjoy the sightseeing part of the drive back and was anticipating a wonderful dinner with Marlee that evening. He had a lot to discuss with Alan. The money being transferred around right now seemed to be related to the Gulf oil situation. Gert had said as much but didn't go into details.

The assumption was that Duncan could piece it all together on reflection.

The Saudis would not be happy with Iran's actions, nor what they planned. The Sauds had one of the most sophisticated spy networks in the Middle East. They would know what Iran planned and be trying to understand what they could do about anything detrimental to Saudi Arabia. War seemed the likely outcome if Iran stayed on the same track. Sunnis would not let the aberrant Shia get away with harming Saudi Arabia. The question is what would the Americans do if war broke out? Secondarily, would the Israelis get involved? Alan would have his hands full trying to work his way through this maze.

The drive started to drag, with both men tired. The trip had been interesting and certainly productive. Marlee was just a bonus, although a beautiful one. A few months ago, he had been thinking seriously about Jessica and then replaced those thoughts with Casey. Now Marlee came into the picture. Unfortunately, in Duncan's line of work, there was little time nor opportunity to maintain a long-term relationship. It would be hard to end what hadn't really started in earnest. When they arrived at the hotel it was already late afternoon. Duncan decided to call Alan again and perhaps try Casey one more time.

"Hi Alan. Let me bring you up to date on my trip with Gert. Also, I am flying to London on Friday and will meet up with Otto. We are both staying at the Piccadilly Hotel. I plan on dinner with him on Saturday evening and maybe sometime on Sunday if possible. Hopefully, he will have more on the transfers to London through Levick. Were you able to find out anything?"

"We found through the NSA that the money was divided between the Caymans and the Bahamas. But I told you that two days ago. No, we are trying to track down whose accounts they went into. Both the NSA and CIA are working on this for me now. I hope to hear at our next meeting on Wednesday. Maybe Otto will know something? In the meantime, I am seeing the President on Tuesday morning per his request. There appears to be a lot of interest in what happened to Haughton, hopefully the V.P. will not be present. Call me anytime if you find anything interesting from Otto. Otherwise, enjoy your last week in Cape Town. Be careful and stay safe. Until we know for sure what is going on I suggest you stay away from our Arab brethren."

"Will do and thanks. I am off to dinner with the young lady who gave us the original information on the transfers. Should be uneventful. Tomorrow is a holiday here, so will probably go to the beach in Camps Bay. It's nice being a tourist for a change. Want a t-shirt?" Alan chuckled.

The ride to Marlee's was uneventful and short. He found himself again looking forward to seeing her with a lot of enthusiasm. Silly really as he knew her for less than a week. Same empty lift to her floor. When her door opened on his knock, she was stunning as usual. This time in a tight-knit dress that accented her magnificent figure.

'Well thank you for the admiring look. I do try." She smiled as she said it.

"A sight for sore eyes. Is it too early to say, 'honey I am home'?"

"No, works for me. Did you have a good trip?"

"Yes, just got back this afternoon. Long drive but quite a beautiful one. I understand why it is called the Garden Route."

"Most people quite like it. Tourists specifically enjoy the ride even though somewhat long. Longer still if you go onto Port Elizabeth. I am glad you are back."

He reached out to her pulling her into him and kissing as he sighed.

"This is just too nice." She took a step back and headed towards the kitchen.

"Your job remains open the wine. Dinner will be ready in twenty minutes. See you on the sofa in a few. Duncan did as he was told, opened and poured two glasses, and headed over to the beautiful view. He could hear Marlee moving pots in the kitchen and the opening and closing of the refrigerator door. The aroma emanating from that room was enticing. Marlee came back with two plates of lamb, potatos and green beans. Steam came from the veggies. She placed the plates on the dining table and came over to Duncan with her hand outstretched. He took it and allowed himself to be led to the table.

"Looks great. Where did you learn how to cook?"

"My Mum was an excellent cook and allowed me to help and learn. She loved Rack of Lamb, so that is one of my favorite dishes. I hope you like it."

'What is not to like? He said it while pulling her again closer to his body.

"Slow down, dinner first, play later. I do not want this food to go bad and you will need your strength. So eat up, plenty of protein for a hungry man."

They both ate and enjoyed the wine. Marlee spoke first.

"I will miss you when you leave. I hope you will come back often and certainly stay in touch." This was said wistfully.

"I have not left yet, so let's clean up afterwards and head back to the bedroom. We can start up where we left off ."

'I do not believe we left off anything but agreed. I am hungry for you."

They both laughed and got up to go to the bedroom. Marlee took a quick turn to the bathroom while Duncan removed his shirt and headed toward the bed. It was a king-sized one, with plenty of room which they needed for all of the thrashing about. She came back again in the silk robe. More beautiful than ever. Her hair framed her smiling face cascading down her chest which was seemingly breathing a little heavier than before. He removed his pants as she came closer.

'To use the cliché, I see you are happy to see me."

"Yes, I am, very happy to see and hold you. Let's lose the robe and get into bed."

After three hours of strenuous activity, they both fell asleep. She was half draped over Duncan's body. Her breathing had calmed as had his. The light from the living room spilled into the bedroom through the partially opened door.

No sounds could be heard other than their combined breathing. Duncan gently stroked her back as she slept, enjoying the sensation of her skin on his. The perfume she used reminded him of gardenias. A beautiful yet subtle smell, mixed in with the previous activity. He knew that smell would never leave his thoughts in the future. A person's association with a smell was rare but like pheromones permanent. In the early morning, the sun began to come through over powering the living room lamp. The bedroom was now well lit and she began to stir.

'What would you like to do today Duncan?"

"I thought we could grab a cab and go over to Camps Bay for a swim and perhaps lunch. What do you think?"

"Good idea, but we will use my Mini. I know a small cafe there that serves South African Crayfish, similar to your lobster but without the claws. Afterward, we can take my Mini and drive down to Cape Point. It is quite a unique drive and worth the hour or so to get there. You will see some antelope and that point where the Indian Ocean meets the Atlantic. We can get some tea there and then back here. I am not letting you go back to the hotel until tomorrow morning." This was said with authority. They both just smiled. Duncan would not argue.

The beach was full. A holiday was in progress. Lots of children running and yelling, playing in the sand and the surf. Mothers casting watchful eyes on their whereabouts. A few young ladies baking in the sun and two surfers riding small waves onto the shore. Marlee and Duncan swam out a few yards in the cold Atlantic. They could see Seals on one side of the beach but stayed well clear of the animals.

" I think we should probably leave now. Have some lunch and then head down to Cape Pont."

"Agreed, it is getting a little crowded here Duncan. But it was fun. Let's get our towels and head to the car. We can park in front of the restaurant, eat, and then off, Swimming makes me hungry."

" You in that Bikini has the same effect on me."

"Slow down boy. Eat first and then drive. "

Duncan scanned the area using his personal threat radar for anyone interested in them. So far nothing but families and a few teenagers hanging about. They gathered up their belongings and headed to the car. The Café was only 600 yards away, but they could and did park in the front. Marlee was correct, the place looked great. Nicely decorated in a seashore motif, but some outdoor seating overlooking the bay. The menus offered Crayfish and some other items, but Marlee insisted on the Crayfish. The dish came with dirty rice on the side and a kind of garlic toast. Hardly health food with all of the drawn butter. Cardiologists would love it. It was the kind of food that allowed you to hear your arteries actually close. Of course, she had changed in the car to a simple sun dress leaving him in shorts and a T-Shirt. The waitress seemed to like his sartorial endeavors. He loved her dress and envisaged what lay beneath it. It had been a great few days except for the weekend with Gert. Tuesday would be back to work for Marlee, and a myriad of emails for Duncan. He thought it might be a good day to hang around the Mosque. He did need to touch base with Otto before their meeting on Saturday. Alan would also be looking for any updates and offer what he had found out through the NSA. The drive to Cape Point was uneventful but interesting. Winding road hugging the sides of a small mountain range. He didn't care where they went as long as he could sit with her. Enjoying the scenery and her. They were back in the flat by 6 pm. Marlee decided to whip up a quick omelet with vegetables. She was indeed a great imaginative cook. Again, Duncan found himself on the sofa looking out over Cape Town and thinking he could get used to this.

"Can you open another bottle of white please? Coffee will be up in a few minutes."

"Sure, but I still can't get over this view. Tomorrow, you have to go back to work and so do I. There are still a few things I need to do in my hotel. I also have to make sure my hotel in London was booked and meeting with Otto confirmed."

"When you do see Otto on the weekend, please thank him for the introduction. It has been a long time since I have enjoyed someone's company as much as yours. Otto is responsible. I owe him for that."

"As do I. Come over here, leave the kitchen alone, and sit with me. "

"I'm learning to hate Tuesdays here."

CHAPTER 21

MONDAY

He smiled as he said it, but some truth to it. This was not how he normally worked. After the bottle was empty, they both headed to the bedroom again. A little too much sun had made them tired. Their enthusiasm however had not been diminished.

Tuesday

Morning came abruptly, but time to head back to the hotel also. Marlee had to go to work. They agreed to repeat that evening, only this time at the Mount Nelson again. Dinner at 7:30, lobby bar as before as the meeting point. She kissed him lightly as he headed out the door to the lift. A cab would be waiting as usual and then off to the Adderley Gardens Hotel.

His room was as he left it. Clothes properly stowed and ready for use if required. Duncan put on his track suit, trainers and started for the lifts when his phone rang.

"Hello".

" Hello Mr. Innes. I have a call on hold here from the USA. Would you like to take it now?"

'Yes, put them through." It was Casey returning his previous calls.

" Sorry we have been playing telephone tag. When are you coming home?"

" Hi Casey, probably the end of next week. I have to go to London on Friday and will be there for about four days. Anything new on your end?"

" Lt. Fischer is still driving me crazy trying to reach you. I have referred him to Alan, but that doesn't seem to satisfy him."

'Any idea what he wants?"

"He is being asked a lot of questions about the men that attacked you at Alan's office and the bomb attempt at Alans home. I answered with what I knew, which is virtually nothing. Please give him a call and get him off my back."

"O.K., I will have Alan kill the inquiry. I will call as soon as I get back. Stay safe."

"You too. What are you into right now. It seems you are the man of the hour and two attempts seem excessive."

"Three, one attempt here in Cape Town last week."

"Duncan, are you all right?"

"Yes I am fine. Someone doesn't like my Yelp reviews."

"Do you know who is behind this?"

"No, but it is starting to look like someone in the States. Right now, I am trying to follow the money that should give some answers."

' I will call you next week when I know for sure when I will return. Thanks for checking on my apartment."

" My pleasure. Brought back some memories. All seems well there. Everything appeared to be in place as I remembered it."

'Ok, tell Fischer I'll call or Alan. As soon as I am back we can do another interview if he wishes. Anything new on facial recognition of the lady in the car""

"Nothing yet, we did have a partial hit on the West Coast at

Customs, however, nothing to follow up on. If we get anything I will text you to call me. Does that work for you?"

" It does indeed, thank you, and stay safe yourself. It's dangerous out there. By the way, if you run into any problems, you can always call Alan. Now that he knows you he will take the call. Remember he is well connected."

"Will do. Have a safe flight to London, enjoy it there, but not too much. "

Wednesday

There goes that guilt feeling again. Duncan started his run towards the docks. Security was remarkably lax in that area of the harbor. Passengers were going back towards one of the cruise ships. A few Ships Chandlers with food and other supplies also passed heading toward the ships. It all looked like a well-oiled machine. When he reached the end of the dock he was running alongside, he turned back in the direction of the Mosque he wanted to visit. On arrival he noticed a large number of men congregating in the front. Some had started to take off their shoes at the entrance. One of the young men turned and looked directly at Duncan. At the same time as recognition dawned he tapped the man next to him and nodded in Duncan's direction. Two others turned and looked in Duncan's direction as well. They seemed to move as one coalescing into one mass and moving toward Duncan. Too many people milling about for them to start anything. But their intent did not seem benign. Instead of entering the Mosque they started in Duncan's direction. He decided that heading back to the main road, Adderely Street would offer fewer oppor-tunities for the men to have a go at him. He turned toward the main road and looked back to see where the other men were. Two had gone to the opposite side of the road and the other trailed closer to him on his side. He had been in a similar situa-tion once in Iraq. He had to make the first move and have surprise on his side. The lead man had pulled out a knife, now held at his side. He was the one that had recognized him at the Mosque. The approach was cautious. They must have heard about their friends and how they ended up in the hospital. All four suddenly stopped moving. It took a moment for Duncan to realize that a Black Mariah police SUV was pulling in behind him.

"Anything wrong sir. We noticed these four seemed to be following you from two blocks back?"

"Nothing officer, just out for a run. I am heading back to my hotel. These guys just seemed to be heading in the same direction."

"Well, be careful and you may want to avoid this area in the future. We have had several robberies here. We wouldn't want you to gain a poor impression of Cape Town. '

'Thank you officer, but I am fine. Beautiful city and I am enjoying every minute of my stay."

"Glad to hear it. Enjoy the rest of the day."

Duncan headed back to the hotel. Time enough for emails, phone calls, and anything else that turned up. The past few days off had been great, but he did need to get back to work. Tonight Marlee, which he looked forward to, but he was getting tired from a lack of sleep. The run today had been good for recharging batteries. Dinner and a night with Marlee would be fantastic, but exhausting nonetheless.

This time no messages at the front desk. Things were quiet. That would change soon enough. First things first, a call to Alan and updates.

"Early morning there again, sorry Alan."

"That's ok, it can't be helped. What's up?"

" You know what we want to do with Gert. Any problems there?"

"Not on my end. We can sneak that through. Let's hope it bears fruit. When do you get the first tranch of information?"

He is supposed to meet up with me Thursday afternoon. I should be able to copy you on anything he brings. That should be a good check on his sincerity. What about your end?"

"Still no joy on the woman we have been searching for, but the V.P. office keeps calling and asking for updates. I suspect that is why the President wants to meet. He is probably feeling the heat from Allyson. I will see him little later and hopefully hear why the interest. As a side note, my new security detail tells me I am being followed around. So far no indication of who is following. Definitely someone in Government as it is always a government car."

"Stay safe, Alan. It is starting to look like we have kicked over a hornet's nest. They tried for me here and they may try for you in D.C. When I get the transfers I will copy you and call from London on Sunday after I have met with Otto. Does that work for you?"

" Great, but you be careful as well. They must know we are looking at the banks or why come after you or I?"

"Agreed, but they knew that from the beginning. It is no surprise that you asked me to look into the two bankers' deaths. While I am not a household name, enough people do know I am your investigative arm. That would be enough if they were trying to hide the why."

"Not as many as you might think. The President and V.P. both know of you, thanks to that exercise in Hong Kong last year. Other than those two and possibly the Chairman of the Joint Chiefs and the NSA you should be unknown."

'Should be that way. By the way, please get Lt. Fischer off Casey's case. He keeps after her on where I am and when will I return. He has become a nuisance. "

"Ok, will do. I had thought that was put to bed. Maybe his boss will know where the heat is coming from?"

"Good, thanks. I'll let Casey know. I did tell her, she could call you anytime for help if needed."

"That's fine. I always liked Casey and she shouldn't be involved in this. Way above her pay grade. I shall see what the President has to say and we can speak on Sunday. If anything comes up in between I will text you to call me ASAP."

"Got it, be careful."

Duncan hung up and opted for a quick shower. A small lunch around the corner at a local café would do nicely. Then back to the hotel send a few emails and get ready for an evening with Marlee. First, an email to Otto confirming his arrival in London. He suggested the Grenadier in Wilton Mews, just off Wellington Circle as a good place to meet for 19:00 hrs. That would be within walking distance from the Picadilly Hotel. Another email to the Restaurant via their website asking for a table for two. Finally a quick call to Jessica, who by now probably forgot all about him. She remained unreachable by phone. An email would have to do for the time being. As he finished up these two emails, the ding of in comings chimed. The dinner reservation was confirmed by Otto and the Grenadier. Next stop was a shower to take the run off his body and then take it easy for an hour. Perhaps a short walk in the City and then off to the Mount Nelson and Marlee. He needed fresh clothes for his trip so decided to use the hotel laundry service. A small paper bag in the hotel closet with a form for the laundry service was inside.

Once outside, having dropped the laundry with the Concierge and ensuring next day's return, Duncan started his walk. No one seemed interested, which was just fine with him. This main road was largely made up of Banks and Department stores. His cell phone jingled as he walked.

"Hello"

"Hi Duncan. Just checking you are still ok and dinner is on tonight."

' Yes, I am all right and looking forward to dinner although more to seeing you again. How is work today?"

"A little odd as Gert came to my office and asked for all of the foreign transfers this past year from Kuwait. Otherwise, all is quiet. See you later and I do miss your company."

"Can't wait and thanks."

They were waiting for him as he left the hotel. Three men, looking somewhat swarthy suggesting a Middle Eastern heritage. One of the men was Assisi the Kuwaiti Banker. Duncan walked directly over to Assisi.

"Anything I can do for you gentlemen?"

The other two backed a little off to either side of the Banker. This area was just a little too public for an open attack.

"Mr. Innes, you may remember me from Frankfurt?"

"I do indeed. We are a little far from Frankfurt right now."

"We are , however I wanted to let you know, I am rather unhappy that your Federal Bank is spending so much time looking into my relationships here and in Germany. Care to explain why this is so?"

"We try to keep track of anyone and everyone that might be involved in supporting terrorism against our interests. I am sure you can understand that. Of course, I could ask why you are in South Africa right now."

"You could indeed, but other than to say I had bank business here with Gert Van Der Merve, I wouldn't comment any deeper that."

CHAPTER 22

THURSDAY

"I trust you were able to complete your task here satisfactorily?"

"Yes indeed, although I keep tripping over you or Alan McDonald. I wonder why?"

"I suggest you ask Alan. Not sure why you are interested in anything I am doing?"

"Just a friendly warning, keep out of my affairs. Kuwait will not take kindly to you snooping around our activities. If you continue, Washington will hear of it and we will see if that is enough to dissuade your interest." As you Americans like to say, have a nice day."

Assisi turned, nodded to the other two men and they all started back in the other direction. The warning had been issued. Now it was up to Duncan to remain vigilant for the other shoe to drop. Thinly veiled threats did not go over well with Duncan. He continued on his walk, carefully checking to see if anyone was following him. Fifteen minutes later Duncan returned to his hotel for another change of clothes and in preparation for his dinner date. As previously, no new messages at the front desk. He tried Jessica again by phone, but she was still out of the office. The weather had hanged to breezy with a possible rain shower. A walk to the Mount Nelson would only take a few minutes and then allow him a quick drink while he waited for Marlee to arrive. No sign of Gert. At the Hotel the bartender was the same man.

"Bells and soda sir?"

"Yes, please make it a double." Duncan enjoyed his drink while watching the front entrance. He was a little early, however the view was entertaining. Tourists wandered in and about. Many had just come from the Gardens and had a little dust on their shoes. One man in particular aroused his interest. He looked out of place. It was the way he carried himself. The man looked like a fighter and moved a little like a boxer. Lithe on his feet and constantly scanning the area for threats. As he got closer, Duncan could see the broken nose silhouette and ears like a rugby player; cauliflower and all. The man paid no attention to Duncan, just walked by and headed towards the hallway and lifts to the rooms above. The bartender suddenly spoke up.

"Do you know who that was?" He pointed to the back of the passerby Duncan had been watching.

"No, can't say that I do. Who is he?"

'That was Jan Devilliers. Our lightweight boxing champ from the Olympics."

"Is he a guest here?"

"Yes, he comes from time to time for about a week. Must be some promotion in town to bring him as a draw."

'Must be a popular guy."

"He is, he will draw a lot of kids and some rugby players as well."

'Will the spectacular young lady you were with last time here be joining you tonight?"

'She will be coming in the next ten minutes or so. I am glad you approve."

"Oh yes, sir. And by the way, there she is coming through the entrance now. Have a great evening."

CHAPTER 23
———————

MOUNT NELSON

Marlee walked the hall to the bar, turning heads as she came closer. She walked up to him, gave him a quick kiss, and sat in front of her newly arrived drink.

"Been waiting long?"

"No, just came in about one-half hour ago for a quick drink before your arrival. I also saw your Jan Devilliers.'

"Really, he is quite a hero in this town. There must be some promotion here. Probably United Tobacco or Rothmans cigarettes doing some light advertising."

" How was your day?"

"Other than waiting for Gert to see me, nothing really exciting. He never did arrive nor call." Marlee jumped in and said,

" I did see Mr. Assisi together with Gert in his office this morning. It was a short visit, but just after Gert had come to me for the copies of the transfers. Perhaps they were related? This visit and request."

"Could be, It would not do for you to be connected to me too closely. Gert knows I know you and we have had dinner a few times, but that is all. "

" I did tell a few people in the bank that I enjoyed dinner with an American acquaintance. No one seemed interested."

"Good, nothing to hide from your end. However, Assisi accosted me by the hotel and tried to warn me off looking into his affairs. I wonder if he was the visitor Monday morning Gert had to see in the City? It is why we came back early. That might explain part of the connection. I am seeing Gert tomorrow hopefully, so I will hear then." They got up and went to the dining room. Both were smiling when the Maitre'd recognized and greeted them. They were shown to the same table over-looking the Gardens. Dinner as in the past was exceptional.

"I am going to miss these dinners with you Marlee."

"Me too, but you will be back. The only question is when.?"

"Yes, as soon as I know, I'll let you know. But, right now, let's go home. By home, I mean your flat."

" By all means. Can you stay tonight?"

"Yes, but I suggest I go back to the hotel early in the morning to catch up on emails etc., and make a few calls prior to my flight mid-day."

"Let's go then now. I do not want to waste any time with you leaving."

Duncan called for the check and placed his credit card on the silver tray. The waiter came back quickly, all done, they could leave. He left a tip in cash and stood up. They both headed to the front entrance. The barman gave a small wave as they passed and was rewarded by a smile from Marlee. She had brought her Mini, so they got in the car and left for Disa Park. The drive was winding and a bit hilly but uneventful. She parked expertly in the lot below her building in an assigned spot. The area was well-lit and showed no one about in the Garage. The view was still fantastic even though an evening fog had started to settle in. Cape Town was famous for the Table cloth that sometimes covered the top of Table Mountain. During the day it would appear quite beautiful. It would be hard for tourists taking the cable car to the top, but worth the ride. They now followed the ritual of opening a bottle of wine from her parent's winery. It had been chilled in the fridge while they were at dinner. She changed; Duncan waited in anticipation. He could not understand why Gert hadn't called. On a whim, he called the hotel and checked for messages.

"Yes Mr. Innes, a courier dropped off an envelope for you. I will hold it here until you return.'

"Thank you, probably early morning when I return."

'Quite alright, I will be here."

"Great, have a good night. See you in the morning."

Duncan did wonder what the envelope might be. Gert had promised a visit personally. As he hung up, Marlee came back into the living room. They made themselves comfortable on the sofa, neither one expecting to be there very long. The cruise ship was gone, but the dock area remained well-lit. He knew he would hate to leave in the morning, but there was a job that needed finishing. The rest of the night was spent saying good bye. The flight tomorrow at mid-day would be arduous. Missing Marlee would not make it any easier. However, he did look forward to seeing Otto again and thanking him for all of the help. How do you thank someone for an introduction to a beautiful girl like Marlee?

" I am going to have to go to the hotel and get my stuff."

" I understand, I can take you to the airport, if you like. I can be at the hotel at 9:45. It is only twenty minutes to the airport. More than enough time and I can see you again. Your bags will fit in the Mini, so no problem."

"Works for me, but what about work?"

"I will tell them I have a dental appointment and be back in two hours. They can do without me for that time."

"I would love that if you do not get into any trouble. I have to leave now, but see you later at the hotel. Drive safely, these drivers here are crazy. Feels a bit like Rome. Everyone racing to the next corner."

'I will, see you in a couple of hours. I will check in at work first. Bye Duncan, as always I loved last night." This said with a radiant smile.

"Me to! I'll grab a cab and be off. Sorry to kiss an run, but a lad has to do what a lad has to do."

He left her at the door and headed for the lift. There were always cabs nearby, so he wouldn't have to wait. That would put him at the hotel by 8 am. Plenty of time to pack and retrieve the envelope. Indeed, there were cabs, Duncan caught one and left for his hotel. Glancing back he thought he saw Marlee in the living room window, but could not be sure. She was hard to leave and he knew he would miss her. The hotel night porter did have the envelope. In his room, he tore it open and found copies of four transfers through the Bank to London. They all were addressed to Levick, so it appeared Gert was holding his end of the bargain. Duncan used his phone's camera, took pictures of each transfer and texted them via What's app to Alan. He emailed a short note that he was on his way to London. He would check in on arrival at Heathrow. A quick shower and then packing up his few belongings and he was ready for his flight. The boarding pass was on his phone in the Wallet section. The laundry he dropped off yesterday was back in his room which made packing much easier. As he finished putting his Dopp kit in the bag the hotel phone rang.

CHAPTER 24

ANOTHER BANKER DOWN

"Duncan, it is awful?" Marlee sounded distraught.

"Marlee, what is the matter?"

"When I came to the office this morning there were police everywhere. My staff were all huddled around my desk with officers going into and out of Gert's office."

"What happened?"

"Gert has been killed. He was found this morning slumped over his desk , shot. There were dollar bills stuffed into his mouth." Who would do such a thing? Can this have anything to do with you and the transfers?"

Duncan was careful with his answers.

"I doubt it. Someone has a beef with Gert and this must have been payback." Duncan immediately thought of Assisi. He had been warned. Somehow, Assisi knew about Gert's deal with Duncan and was sending a message.

"The police are interviewing everyone here, one by one. I cannot take you to the Airport, sorry. You will have to take a cab. There is no way to know how long this will take. The cleaning lady that found him is really upset as is my staff.

"No problem a taxi will do fine. I will call you before boarding and again from London when I land. I know I will miss you. Try to take it easy."

" I will miss you too. I had a wonderful week or so with you. Please come back when you can. After all, who is going to open my wine in the evening?"

" For the police, you have done nothing wrong. Answer their questions. I am sure they will get the picture that Gert was not a popular guy around town. Information about sharing the transfers are not necessary for them to know. In any case, I doubt that had anything to do with what happened. Something bad has caught up to Gert. Who knows what that could be?"

"Agreed, thanks Duncan, sorry about the airport. I did want to see you again, but I cannot leave my staff here to face this alone. The Bank chairman will be here shortly, speak with the troops, and ensure Bank business continues with minimum disruption. Right now an Officer is waving in my direction. Have a good flight, I will miss you." She hung up.

Duncan texted Alan a short note, 'Gert has been murdered in his office. I suspect Assisi is involved. I will call from London'.

The boarding process was simple. Just before he got on the plane, he made a quick call to Marlee, but she did not pick up. The flight was relatively full, but Business Class made that acceptable. He had one passenger sitting next to him. The man looked like a salesman, which proved to be true. There ensued a short conversation on sales in the RSA and banking. Nothing suspicious, just an arcane conversation of travelers. The Stewardesses brought hot towels offered drinks and went through their safety spiel. The flight left on time, so for the next twelve hours there really was nothing to do but sleep or watch terrible movies. The obligatory Pasta or rubber Chicken was served two hours into the flight. Breakfast was promised one hour before landing. It sounded more like a threat. One glass of wine would have to do. Too much reminded him of Marlee and her evening wine. From experience, Duncan knew long-distance relationships were almost impossible. Jessica was a proof statement for the foregoing. He had not been able to reach her for the entire week and half he was gone. Even contact with Casey was spotty. The only one consistent in his life was Alan. He could always be reached. For some, a sad state of affairs. For Duncan this was normal. The salesman next to him fell asleep. This allowed Duncan to go over in his head, uninterrupted past occurrences. Assisi was the key to all that was happening. Somehow Kuwait was the nexus of the attacks, killings, and problem Duncan and Alan were trying to solve. Maybe Otto could shed some light on the current events. If this all came back to a Middle East problem, what was it? So far all of the transfers amounted to close to 75 million dollars. What was that buying?

CHAPTER 25

LONDON

On landing at Heathrow, Duncan began thinking about whom to call first? He really wanted to check on Marlee, but also needed to hear from Alan what the status of all the enquiries to date produced. Marlee won the toss. He dialed her home number first as it was Saturday morning in Cape Town.

"Good morning Marlee. I am at the Airport in London. Are you ok?"

" I am fine. The police stayed at the bank for four more hours after you left. The Chairman ordered an audit by an outside firm to make sure Gert hadn't been up to anything. That will take at least four days. Forensic auditing is a long involved process. I doubt they will find anything but the Banks Board wants to be sure. I missed you last night. How was the flight?"

"Boring, but I am glad you are okay. Stay safe. Whoever killed Gert may be interested in his friends or colleagues. I will call again tomorrow morning, your time. You may want to stay with a girlfriend tonight. I am not happy that you are alone. And I miss you as well."

"I'll be fine. Today is an easy day as is tomorrow. I will probably drive out to Stellenbosch and see some friends there. I would have liked to introduce you to them, maybe next time. Go to your hotel, get some sleep. You must be exhausted."

"Will do, stay near a lot of people if possible. Let me know if you hear the Police turned up anything. Have an uneventful day Marlee. I'll be thinking of you. I see Otto tonight."

"Please say hello from me. Also, my thanks for the introduction."

"I certainly will, and second the thanks, big time. Talk to you tomorrow."

"Bye now, Duncan, be careful."

The Picadilly Hotel had seen better days, but still a Grande Old Dame. The check-in process was simple. He had stayed here many times in the past.

Time to call in to Alan.

"I have arrived in London. Anything new on your end?"

"Yes, the meeting with the President went well. He asked to be remembered."

"Thank you, what else did he have to say?"

" The Haughton murder was still on his mind. Apparently, the V.P. Allyson is not happy with how slow the investigation is going. I tried to bring him up to date and told him we think it is related somehow to the Middle East. He did say, you were becoming a problem for him. The V.P. took some complaints about your meddling in Kuwaiti affairs from their ambassador. I assume that came from Assisi?"

"Probably, as I texted you, Assisi had accosted me in Cape Town and tried to warn me off further investigations on Kuwait. Assisi mentioned you, Alan by name."

"The President explained that the V.P. spends a lot of time with the Kuwaitis as part of his assigned task of reporting to the President on any issues in the Mid-East, This is a throwback to when the V.P. was the Secretary of State under the previous administration. I assume that is the route taken to get you to back off."

"Sounds about right. Any idea what the problem with Gert was and why was he killed? The dollars stuffed in his mouth suggest the U.S.A. connection, perhaps a message?"

"Well, we now know the transfers all went to numbered accounts in the Caymans and the Bahamas. A treaty does exist with the Bahamas and the U.S. to pursue money launderers and tax cheats. But breaking numbered accounts and getting the names of the holder is very difficult. The FBI is currently researching that connection on our behalf. Still, I am trying to keep a lid on this. The last thing I want to do is spook someone into going underground. See what Otto has to say and we can go on from there. Stay safe Duncan, if the president gets involved it is already too big. And by the way, I have a lead on our young lady. She has definitely changed her appearance significantly. Our facial recognition systems caught her in D.C. last week. We are still trying to get a name and address, but the computer geeks are very certain she is the same person. I am going to text you a picture. Somewhat grainy but you can make the face out fairly well. She is really good-looking. We are trying to run the picture through some of the known countries with plastic surgeons. My guess is Brazil , but it could be Venezuela. The same computer boys are hacking into very database they can find in both countries. We are comparing the old picture from Hertz to the current one. Now it is just a question of when our thirteen-year-old hackers get lucky. I am glad we have them, but wonder where they developed their skills."

"Your picture just came through. I do recognize her."

"How, can that be?"

"She sat next to me in D.C. at the Whale. We chatted for a few minutes and then we both left. I was taking a call and she ducked out the side door. I saw her leave. You are right, she is quite a stunner. Most of the men at the bar seemed impressed. No, my question is what are the odds she comes to our bar?"

"That is a little too close for comfort. Be careful Duncan."

"Will do. I have to change and get ready to meet Otto at the Grenadier."

"You still love that place?"

"I do. Ever since I ran into that Real Estate agent that gave me a guided tour of the house across from the Pub it has been a favorite."

"Give my best to Otto and thanks."

They hung up, Duncan showered again and changed his clothes getting ready to walk to the Grenadier. It was a warm evening so a simple long sleeve shirt would be enough. Again he was pleased he had the foresight to launder his clothes before leaving Cape Town.

The lobby was packed, but a quick scan produced no visible threats. It only took ten minutes to walk over to Wilton Mews. It was still early but a small crowd had spilled over onto the Mews itself with pints in hand. The pub sported layers of flowers on the windows and banister on the walk up to the front door. An inviting look for anyone. He climbed the stairs and checked in with the hostess. Otto had not arrived. He purchased a Pint of lager and went back outside. Nursing the beer in waiting for Otto seemed like a good idea. Being already tired from the long flight, he saw no need to make it worse by downing too much beer too early. A few patrons were female and they did look at Duncan with some smiling. For the moment, however he had no eyes for anyone other than Marlee.

"Well Duncan, I see nothing has changed. The ladies are still smiling at you!" Otto had come up to his side.

"Thanks, Otto but I am not interested. I can't be sure if I

should thank you for the introduction to Marlee or punch you for it.'

'Let's stay with thank you. She emailed me this morning also expressing thanks. I take it you two had a glorious time together. I am jealous, she is really a beautiful lady. My wife would be very unhappy if she knew I was a friend of Marlee's. You know how women are? But, after all, we are work friends"

" I understand, and yes we did have a wonderful time. Totally unexpected, but I will think about her a lot. "

"You recognize, of course, your job does not exactly support anything serious and there is certainly the distance to consider."

"I am glad I could bring you two together. I quite like Marlee and have become friends with her over the years. Think of this introduction as payback for your past support."

"I do, but thanks anyway and I am well aware of that. She spoke highly of you. Now to a bit of business, have you found out anything about the transfers?"

"I have. 'Levick's number two is not exactly a friend but close enough. We have done a lot of business together in the past. He suggested that there was something off about all three transfers he was aware of last year. He had pointed that out to Levick, who told him to bugger off. "

"Why?"

" Apparently, he believes that the transfers were political."

"How so and to whom?"

"As you know the whole world has become paranoic. No one wants to be involved in anything that can come back and bite them in the proverbial rear."

"Understood Otto, but do we know who the transfers were destined for at this time?"

" His understanding was that the money to both the Caymans's and Bahamas were wired to numbered, unnamed accounts. Levick had warned Haughton. We have information that Haughton had found the accounts were managed by ALLTEL, a US finance NGO company. That company specialized in supporting rural telephone systems for the under privileged. ALLTEL on doing research turned out to be the V.P.'s son pet project. He apparently runs the company in Ridgewood, N.J. as an NGO. Christian Allyson has received large sums of money in the past. He usually claims consulting work or some such to account for it and points to his NGO Status.. I do not know if he pays taxes on this, nor where the final disbursements end up. There is a limit to this information availability. I was surprised we even found out that Christian was the holder of the accounts even though indirectly."

"In short do not ask how?"

"Yes, I couldn't tell you without compromising my source. It also appears that ALLTEL manages and supports a SuperPac for D.C. politicians. They distribute large amounts of cash on behalf of their pet campaigns.

"Now the question is, what do we do with this information? I will have to tell Alan what we know. Any chance for proof or is this all on the Q.T?"

"Right now, it is all part of the old boy's network. It has to remain that way."

'Thanks Otto. This does answer a question Alan and I had on the V.P.s interest in all of this. Ever since Haughton and Levick were killed, the V.P. has shown great interest on where we were in the investigation. If his son is somehow involved I understand the interest. Perhaps the V.P. wants to run interference for his son. Keep the money Flowing would be a priority. The sums are huge and I am sure that Christian would not want this to stop coming. We have motive if Christian believes that Haughton or Levick are going to blow this all up.

'Be careful Duncan. You are at the top of the administration or close enough. Blow back could be fatal."

"Agreed, but blow back from whom? The V.P., his son, or someone else?"

"Have the conversation with Alan. He is connected and may be able to help decipher what is going on. I can't understand what the Kuwaitis would want from Christian. Where is the gain? They are spending a lot of money here,there must be a reason. What is it? Maybe it is, as simple as ALLTEL ats aa lobbyist for the gulf States. They must be concerned at waht iran is doing and possible coming disasters to their coffers. Saudrabia could also be adding money to the pot just using Kuwait as the means to effect transfers. Buying influence is nothing new, but with a possible war with Iran imminent having the Americans as their back up makes sense. The Gulf States and Saudi Arabia are dependent on U.S. military aid. That aid has to keep flowing to be a deterrent to Iran."

The hostess chose that minute to come out and escort them to their table. The restaurant part of the Pub was now packed. Too many people, too close to have a meaningful conversation without being overheard. They both ordered wine, and the lamb. The lamb reminded Duncan of Marlee's lamb. The potatoes were a little undercooked, but otherwise perfect. When they finished, they both had coffee, no dessert.

"It has been great catching up Otto, Thanks for the information, I will let you know what happens. Right now, I am tired from the flight and need to get back to the hotel and get a night's sleep."

"Understood, and thanks for dinner. I am sure Alan won't scream at the expense considering the information I gave you." He smiled as he said it.

" No problem Otto, want to meet again tomorrow?"

" I can't Duncan, have meetings all day and then back to Frankfurt tomorrow evening. Text me if there is anything you need and think I can help. It was nice seeing you again, and if you speak with Marlee give her my regards."

"Will do. I will call you next week if I find anything new. I think I will be flying back home on Monday to Washington. That assumes Alan wants me there."

"Be careful Otto, you heard what happened to Gert or?"

"I did indeed. So far no one has been arrested. Our man in Cape Town was aware of the murder but had no details. If I hear anything I will let you know."

"Thanks, Otto and have an uneventful trip home tomorrow."

They both left the Pub. It was a short walk back to Wilton Row, where Otto could pick up a taxi.

Duncan turned left walking past the Wellington Monument and headed back to the Piccadilly Hotel. The night had turned cooler but still pleasant. Cars careened around the Monument Circle. It was always a busy thorough fare. Their farewells had been brief, but both were happy to have renewed their friendship. Duncan now had a lot to think about. The V.P.'s involvement, through his son, would be a problem for him and Alan. The so-called 'can of worms' was being opened. Now for his phone call to Alan bringing him up to date. This should be interesting, to say the least. On return to the Hotel Duncan called Alan at his home. After an update of everything that Otto had told him was passed along, Alan said, "We need to check more into what ALLTEL is up to and who is behind this firm. If the V.P.s son, Christian Allyson is indeed the principal here. This will become a political nightmare. The V.P. and his son certainly know they must be registered as a lobbyist to support any politicians here. Not doing that is a crime in itself. Why don't you come home asap? I will look into ownership of ALLTEL and have that information available when you arrive."

Duncan jumped in, "I will try and catch a flight tomorrow

back to D.C. I will check in with you when I arrive at Dulles. See if you can get a list of employees of Altel, that might be useful."

"Will do Duncan. Have a safe flight. Speak tomorrow when you arrive. In the meantime, I will book you a flight from Heathrow and text you the information. Your documents, and boarding pass will be on the text. Have a safe light."

Duncan retired early and tried to sleep off the past two days. Tomorrow would be another very long day. He tried again for a quick call to Marlee and explained to her answering machine that he would be flying to the USA tomorrow and therefore unreachable. On waking up the next day, a text confirmed his 12:30 pm flight to D.C. with British Airways from Heathrow, terminal 5 to Dulles. His arrival time in D.C. would be 2 pm. The time to leave was now. He could not afford to slowly get ready. Traffic to Heathrow was always a problem and he needed to be on time or miss the flight.

Four hours later he was sitting in his First Class seat. Alan probably couldn't get Business Class so opted for what was available. Two emails had also arrived from D.C, while he slept. The first from Alan was a listing of employees at ALLTEL. Duncan did not know how he got this information so fast, but it would make things easier. Three men with Irish and German names were listed as sales and marketing people: a Hans Ritter, Erich Kochan and Sean Riley made the list. . One woman was also listed as a secretary. No other employees on the list. Christian Allyson was however shown as the sole owner and CEO of this NGO and it was registered as such. A brief description of the company's work to supply cell phones at low cost to rural communities. The idea was to give communities without phones, at least one central point where cell phone service could be accessed. ALLTEL was licensed in many countries to offer their service. They included Iraq, Syria, India and

Pakistan. Duncan put the three names in his cell phone for later reference and the company address in Ridgewood, N.J.. When he landed in D.C. his first call was to Alan.

"I have arrived. Checking emails and saw your notes on the three employees and Christian as an owner. Thank you, might not be important. Can you get any other information on the three employees? In particular last jobs and for whom. What function did they have?"

"I will check Duncan. So far our data has come through friends at the I.R.S. .Some danger here. There also appears to be a connection to a Superpac that is funded by ALLTEL, very hard to prove, but the rumor mill supports this. " We are rattling trees. I received another call just a few minutes ago from the V.P. asking for an update on your activities and where you were. I said you hadn't reported in as yet, but when you returned you would call. He sounded miffed that his call produced so little information. "

"Well, hold him off for now. I need to check up on Christian and these three employees. I will be in the City proper tomorrow after lunch with Casey for a quick bite and then come to you. Home or your office?"

"Let's make it my office. My home building manager is still upset that we blew up part of his garage. "

"Fine, see you about 2:30 depending on traffic."

"Stay safe Duncan, I am sensing we are getting closer to wrapping this all up, I hope." Duncan hung up and took an Uber to his apartment. The drive took almost an hour and not even rush hour. Casey agreed to meet for lunch the next day at the deli by Dupont Circle. She sounded pleased to hear from Duncan and said she looked forward to catching up at the deli. They left it for 12:30 as a good time for both. That gave Duncan the morning to get back into his workout routine. Get the cobwebs out of his head from the flights. Short text from Marlee hoping all was okay. She would be back home that evening. She hoped she would hear from him. It was nice being back in his own apartment. Everything looked in order, some mail had piled up, but mostly advertising.

He used the time to research the names Alan had supplied. No hits on LinkedIn or Facebook for any of them That was a long shot anyways. He looked at the website of ALLTEL which described, with pictures, phones in India in small villages. The site made ALLTEL seem like a typical NGO supporting poor third world countries towns. A picture of Christian Allyson was placed in 'About Us'. Ritter, Kochan and Riley were also listed with picture and stated as support people representing ALLTELs on going services to bring communications to the poor. His phone rang as he went through the many advertisements that had been piled up in his mailbox.

CHAPTER 26

WASHINGTON

"Hello."

"Hi Duncan." Marlee's unmistakable cheerful voice.

"Hi Marlee. All well in South Africa?"

"Oh yes. I have spent two days in Stellenbosch with friends, but now home. How are you and how was your trip?"

"The trip was tiring but otherwise all good. Otto sends his warm regards. He did mention he was jealous of me, but I know he loves his wife."

"I certainly hope so. I have always liked Otto since I first met him some years ago. I have not met his wife, but assume she must be nice."

"She is indeed. Very German, all by the book, but a great lady. I am glad to hear your voice and that you are okay. Have you heard anything more about Gerts murder? What are the Police saying or are they quiet.?"

"Very quiet right now I do not think they know anything if I believe SABC TV. The Forensic Audit is now going on, but nothing so far. I will be back in the office tomorrow. I did take a call from the Chairman Devilliers yesterday. And I have a promotion. They want me to take Gert's job. It makes some sense in that I am the next in line there anyway. Hopefully, I will not end up as Gert."

"Not if I can help it you will not. Let's do this, I will call again tomorrow, and you can tell me about the job and anything new happening in the Bank. Keep an eye on the news for any news they may offer."

"Will do, but I think that ship has sailed as well. I did tell the police that a Mr. Assisi had been in the office just before Gert was killed. They did not seem interested. They knew that Assisi was a Kuwaiti from Mr. Devilliers. They had asked the nature of Mr. Assisi's visits and Devilliers told them about the Banks transfers and that they were a normal service offered by the bank. That seemed to satisfy them. Mr. Devilliers later told me all of this and said if the police came back I should tell them whatever they wished to know without compromising the Bank's integrity. For the time being, I was in charge of all Bank security and continue to be in charge of all wire transfers. In particular, I should pay attention to whatever the Kuwaitis wanted. They represented a large income source for the Bank. I promised I would and thanked him for the vote of confidence. I do wish you were here right now. It's all a bit confusing, every-thing is happening so fast. "

"I will try and get out to you as soon as I can. Do your job, you have nothing to fear. I am sure the Bank loves you, like everyone else that meets you."

"Thank you, Duncan. I will try and be as normal as possible. I do need to her from you whenever you can call. You have a calming effect on me and an exciting one."

" I certainly hope so. Take it easy today, I will call tomorrow.

Have a good night, sweet dreams. I will be dreaming of you. Bye now."

"Goodbye, Duncan." The line went dead. He hoped he was right that she was safe. He needed a good nights' sleep. Seemed to be a recurring problem lately. The following morning, Duncan got up early and went outside for a run. Five miles should do it after so little activity the past few days. Traffic in the city was light. Two other runners passed him by, both had earbuds and seemed to be listening to music as they ran. He often thought this was dangerous as you never knew if a car was about to plow into you or a bicycle. At the 2.5-mile spot, Duncan turned and headed back to his apartment. A shower, shave and new clothes would round out the morning. Still no visible threats in the area. Hopefully, it would stay that way. He had about an hour to get to the deli and meet up with Casey. Again his phone rang as he reached his floor.

"Good morning Duncan. I want to bring you up to speed. The V.P. has called yet again. The president has also asked for another meeting with both of us for this afternoon at 5 pm. A pass will be at the main gate for you. I will also try an arrive at the same time. I'll see you then."

"Anything new on our three friends from ALLTEL"

"Sorry no. They are on the Company's Website so I got a look at them. As advertised they represent sales and marketing for ALLTEL. Christian is listed as the CEO owner. I would like to take a closer look at them. I will probably head out to New Jersey after our meeting with the president and go on Wednesday or Thursday. I want to drop in on their office unannounced. Any objections?"

"Not right now. Just be careful. I do not have the same reach in New Jersey as I have here. Caution please!"

" Although be very careful. If ALLTEL is involved in all of this, your turning up may spook them. Someone trying to kill us suggests they or their cohorts are already spooked. Let's get through what the President wants and move on from there."

He caught an Uber to the Deli where he was to meet Casey. So far no threats presented themselves. Things seemed quiet. That in itself was a bad sign. Too much was happening behind the scenes. Gert being murdered suggested more was to come. Perhaps the President had some new plan or already knew about the V.P.'s involvement. That would make him complicit. Not a happy thought. Duncan needed someone high up to be on the side of the angels.

Once inside the deli, Duncan saw Casey again eating a bagel and what looked like lox. H smiled at the waitress and sat down next to Casey.

"Hi, you look happy."

"I am, as I was hungry. They really have the best bagels outside of New York. Tell me about your trip."

Duncan launched into an abbreviated version of the trip, with some details of Assisi and the Shia crescent of Power concept. He did not talk about Marlee but did mention Gerts murder. "

"Way above my pay grade Duncan. Are we any closer to the killer of Haughton? Lt. Fischer reaches out to me daily on your status and whereabouts. He is like a bulldog with a bone. He is not going to let that go. You do need to have a word with him for everyone's sake. Once the interview is over, he may be molli-fied somewhat. But I doubt it."

"Casey, we re getting closer. We know that this is all related to the Middle East. The Kuwaitis are involved, the Sauds and the Iranians, but how is still open. Alan is running that down now. Th short answer I someone keeps trying to kill me. Happened in Cape Town which I narrowly escaped. More from the incompetence of the attackers than my prowess. The lady that killed Haughton, or so we believe, is still on the loose. But she could turn up anywhere. Listen, I have to cut this short as I have another meeting with the President tis afternoon. I do not want to be late."

"I understand Duncan. Lets walk to my car, I can give you a ride to the White House if you like?"

"Thanks and yes. I assume you are on the circle o nearby?"

"I am indeed. Just five minutes from here. We cross the center of the Circle and we are there., so lets go."

They both stood up and headed outside. Casey slipped her arm into his and they walked onto the circle. She suddenly stopped and yelled 'Gun'. In the same breath, she pulled her service revolver and fired at someone to Duncan's right.

The sound or her gun covered the shot from the as yet unseen assailant. Duncan looked right and saw a woman falling to the pavement with a gun at her side. Casey also went down. She had been hit in the left shoulder. He reached down to her to see how badly she had been hit. There was a general chaos of sound around them as people screamed and started to run away. Casey was bleeding from her shoulder but not pulsating blood. A good sign that no major artery had been hit. A woman with a baby carriage started to pass by and Duncan stopped her.

"Do you have a diaper in that baby bag?"

'Yes, do you need it?"

"I do, it will staunch the flow of blood from this woman's shoulder." He took the offered diaper and placed it over the wound. At the same time he pulled his cell phone, called nine one one and reported the shooting.

'Nine one one, I have a gunshot victim here on the Southeast corner of Dupont Circle. There is a second victim a few yards from me. Please call the police and tell them one of the victims with me is Casey O'Brian a D.C. police officer. We need an ambulance asap."

The diaper was filling up with blood when the first ambulance arrived. Two paramedics jumped out and started to work on Casey. She was drifting in and out of consciousness. Three police cruisers also appeared. Two officers came to Duncan who was still kneeled by Casey.

"Please stand up Sir, and put your hands on top of your head."

Duncan complied immediately not wanting to be shot by a nervous cop. Two more police officers turned up and ran over to the other victim. One felt for a pulse but shook his head no. Duncan could now see her face and immediately recognized the girl from the Whale and Alan's picture of the killer. Casey had saved him from being shot. Now she was lying on a Guerney.

'Where are you taking her?"

"Nearest hospital is George Washington University Hospital. She is in good hands and the bleeding has abated. Do you have her name?"

"Yes, she is Casey O'Brien of D.C. Police." The two police officers with Duncan said, "ok, now we go to the Station. What is your name and do you have any I.D.?"

Duncan said he wanted to reach into his pocket and pull his wallet. The I.D. confirmed his name, and address plus status as a special investigator for the Federal Reserve. That I.D. made him a type of police officer, so he was treated with more respect. The handcuffs were removed and he was escorted to the cruiser and onto the main Station.

"He told the Desk Sergeant to call Lt. Fischer who would be interested in this encounter. A small interview room was opened and he was offered a cup of coffee. One hour later Fischer turned up.

"Here and under these circumstances are not exactly how I expected to see you again M. Innes.'

"I understand. At least part of your caseload is cleared."

"How so?"

"The other victim on the circle is your killer of Haughton. If you match up her face with your facial recognition system, you will see they are the same people. Casey recognized the woman had a gun and got off her shot at the same time as the killer. Their bullets must have passed one another. But for Casey's speed, I would not be here for this chat. I would like to check , on Casey please. She is at the University Hospital."

The Paramedics said you saved her life with the diaper trick. She is being operated on now. A bullet is lodged in her left shoulder and needs to be removed. I am told she will recover but may be a bit stiff for quite a while. Your call to Alan McDonald on the way here has brought some relief for you. I understand you are in the middle of an investigation and Casey was part of it. Alan McDonald is on the way here to pick you up. He says he has duplicate photos of the woman in the Circle that tried to shoot you and I can have them for evidence. This is all from facial recognition software. Someday, you are going to have to explain to me what this is all about."

"It is a long story and almost unbelievable."

Alan McDonald chose that moment to come into the interview room.

"Are you okay Duncan?"

"I am, but worried about Casey. She took out our Whale lady prior to me being taken out. Her speed and reaction to a real threat was very impressive."

"I understand you both got lucky. Lt. Fischer here are the photos, I promised. It looks like one part of the cases will be closed going forward."

"One part?"

" Lt. We still have the English Banker Levick to deal with, but I suspect the two cases are related."

"What are you two involved with now? I am only interested in Haughton, as my case. An English banker does not fit into my investigation." Fischer continued to shake his head.

"Believe it or not Lt. the two cases are related. I think when we look into all of this deeper we will find the lady was involved in the English banker's death and possibly a South African's death as well. She has been a very busy girl. Duncan, we have to leave. Our appointment for this afternoon is still on so we have to go, any objection Lt. Fischer to our both leaving now?" "No, but stay available, should I have follow-up questions. I will also call the hospital and see how Casey O'Brien is doing. From what they told me before, she is probably out of the O.R. and doing fine. Try not to shoot anyone Mr. Innes today. You are keeping me busy. I need a day off from shootings and bombings."

Duncan took an Uber to the Hospital. He wanted to check on Casey. The receptionist at the entrance gave him her room number. He took the elevator to her floor, found the room and looked in on Casey strapped to a harness over head keeping her shoulder elevated. She was asleep., probably for the best. He entered the room, but she remained asleep. Slightly snoring. Alan arrived and said we have to go and see the President.

"Okay, but I hate to leave her like this.'

"Understood, but the President takes precedent right now." Alan ushered Duncan out of the room and to the waiting car. "You can come back after our meeting. Are you still planning on going to New Jersey?"

"Yes I am. "

"We should discuss what we are going to tell the President."

"Agreed, but I think we should let him take the lead. He called the meeting after all."

"Ok, fine by me, but I am getting really unhappy with these constant attempts on my life. When they start on my friends it has gone too far."

Chapter 27

The President

They pulled up to the main entrance to the White House. A guard with a clipboard came up to the car took their I.D.'s and checked them against his list of authorized visitors.

"Gentlemen, you are good to go in. Park up there by the entrance, I.D. badges will be waiting for you at the small building on the right. Please wear them at all times in the building."

"Thank you, we will do." A uniformed Marine met them at the door and escorted them into the building. They were taken to the Oval Office where the President was sitting on one of the two facing sofas.

"Good afternoon Alan and to you Duncan. Thank you for coming. I was told about the shooting on Dupont Circle this morning. Is the young officer that was shot doing ok now?"

Duncan chose to answer, "Yes, sir. She was operated on to remove the bullet but is now in a room recovering. The Doctor told me she will be fine, although complete use of her arm may be limited. Time will tell."

"Tell me what happened," said the President.

Duncan recounted the events of the morning including Casey's shooting by the 'Whale Lady'. He did say it was her or us. Fortunately, Casey was quicker and a better shot.

"Any idea of who was behind this?" the president looked to Alan for an answer.

"We have our suspicions, but nothing we can prove as yet sir."

Well, I called you in as I am getting constant calls from the Kuwaiti Ambassador about both of your activities. Add to those calls the V.P. Allyson also jumping in on the bandwagon. As you know from his days at State, I put him in charge of keeping an eye on the Middle East and in particular Saudi Arabia and Kuwait along with the other Gulf States. I believe Alan you two were friends for many years?"

"That is true Sir, however, we more or less fell out of touch. We move in different circles and I can't afford having too much oversight in what I do for the Federal Reserve. There are times when I have to ask Duncan and others to do things that shouldn't come out to the light of day. Think back to the Hong Kong Business last year and that will make sense. We both did meet with the V.P. a few weeks ago on the Haughton issue, but nothing came of it." Alan shrugged as he said this.

"What are you not telling me Alan, or maybe Duncan should answer that?"

Duncan looked at Alan and then back to the President. It was hard not to answer a question from him under any circumstance.

'Sir, I am happy to tell you what I think, but cannot prove it as yet. You may not want to hear this."

"Go ahead and tell me. I can solve problems I am aware of but can't do a thing about what I do not know."

'Yes sir. What I have since the death of Haughton is as

follows, Haughton was aware of money transfers from South Africa to London and then on to the Caymans and the Bahamas. That awareness probably caused him his life. "

"How much money are you talking about?"

Alan responded, "to date over 75 million dollars"

"That is a lot of spare change. Where did it go?" This time Duncan took the lead,

"To the Vice President's son Christian Allyson via his NGO ALLTEL in New Jersey. Still haven't been able to prove it other than hearsay. Before you ask sir, ALLTEL also supports a Super Pac that feeds both parties funds from time to time."

"Where did the money originate and how do you know where it ended?"

"The money comes from Kuwait. Probably funds comingled with Saudi and Gulf State funds. Our sources are confidential but within the Bank of England, the EU Central Banks, and the South African National Bank. We know a Mr. Assisi is in charge of this from Kuwait. All of this information was confirmed by Duncan in the last two weeks on his trips to London and Cape Town. Mr. Assisi has accosted Duncan and warned him off. This was followed by the V.P. office asking us to lay off."

"The lady on Dupont Circle was a contract killer who meant to take me out. She missed and got Casey, the officer that was shot. We believe that we will be able to prove over time, that she was behind the Levick killing in Brighton, England, and Gert van der Merve in South Africa. Three bankers in a row. Multiple attempts on our lives in my office, home, and in South Africa when Duncan was down there collecting information. The assumption is Haughton, who knew Levick found out about the transfers and figured out who was behind them and that information became his death sentence.

"What you are saying is Christian Allyson is acting as an Agent for Saudia Arabia, the Gulf states, and Kuwait."

" Yes sir, that is what we now believe."

"Why, what is in this for him?"

'Actually, quite a lot. He seems to have an endless source of funds going through his accounts. He also has serious access to what is happening next in the oil-producing countries. The so-called Shia Crescent of Power is a real thing. If Christian can influence our behavior, perhaps through his father or Super Pac recipients the ability to make millions on the commodity exchanges is huge. The Mid-East picks up friends and has a constant source of information on what we are doing and planning going forward. They can also interfere with our actions towards Iran. Think in terms of Iran closing off access to and from the Gulf, and what happens to oil prices. Two big winners: Iran and Russia. This of course depends on the building of a pipeline to the Mediterranean. How long the Gulf is closed affects prices everywhere. Christian has himself a money machine without limits.'

" Is the V.P. in on this scheme?"

"By inference only. Nothing we can prove, but he is certainly heavily invested in shutting us down, meaning Duncan and myself. Would this stand up in court, probably not, but the Court of Public Opinion could bring your Presidency down if it leaked out that we were being manipulated by Middle Eastern Countries from within the Government. There really is no other explanation that explains the facts as we know them."

" Thank you, Alan and Duncan for bringing this to me. Please continue your investigation and by all means, find out if the V.P. is indeed involved beyond his son's behavior if possible. I will deal with the V.P. myself, so keep this to yourselves. Please get back to me as soon as possible if you find out anything more concrete. Thank you again for coming by. I realize that this is a real burden for you to quietly carry, but for the good of the Country, this must remain quiet. Feel free to call the number on this card, anytime you have something I should know or need any help this office can offer. Duncan put the card in his wallet and hoped he would never need it. They both said their good-byes and headed for the parking lot. Each gave up their ID badge at the door and went to the car.

"Would you drop me off at the hospital please, I want to check on Casey.?"

'Certainly. It's al little late, but La Perla is just around the corner. Care for some dinner after you see Casey?"

"Sure, just drop me off at the hospital, I can walk the short distance to the restaurant. See you there. I will not be long as Casey will need her rest."

The car let Duncan out at the side entrance and left for La Perla. He made his way up to her floor finding her awake this time.

"How are you, Casey?" She had a big smile on her face.

'Certainly happy to see you are alright. I wasn't sure and no one would tell me here. I am fine, thanks to you. You took out the lady sent to kill me and also the killer of the Federal Reserve Banker. That ought to be worth a medal or two.

I am glad to hear it. By the way, Lt.Fischer stopped by. He told me about your conversation at the precinct. Thanks. There will still be a shooting investigation on the Circle incident, but it will not be a problem. My Captain also stopped by about a half hour ago. I passed the Leutenants exam. So it appears I have to be shot to get promoted. I will still be at the same precinct, but nice pay raise, and remain on the homicide squad, but now ranked."

Duncan smiled at her and patted her good shoulder. "We will have to celebrate when you get out of here. What are they telling you for a prognosis?"

"I will be good to go in a week. Then it is rehab for six weeks to get strength and coordination back. The shooting is considered in the line of duty as I was bringing you in to speak with Lt. Fischer. I saw no good reason to disavow that. I trust you agree?"

"I do, but let's not have you take any more bullets on my behalf. It is hard enough to keep friends in this town without losing the few I have to random shooters."

A dinner tray was wheeled in as Duncan was relating what had happened that morning. He filled in the blanks of her memory. Trauma always left things a bit vague. Her dinner looked like mystery meat surrounded by non-descript vegetables. Duncan believed that all hospital dieticians went to a special school to learn how to remove any hint of flavor from hospital trays. They did this schooling for an average of four years as well. It was a talent shared by all of them. Rather like what the Brits do to steak. There was no empathy for patients.

"I am rather tired Duncan. Thank you for stopping by, but I need to get some sleep."

'No problem get well soon. I will try and come back tomorrow, but I may have to go to New Jersey for Alan. In any case I have your room phone number so I will call. Have a good night. Till tomorrow."

She smiled but closed her eyes. Thankfully the lady that had put her here was no longer among the living. No need to worry about someone attacking Casey. She was now out of harm's way. Duncan left the hospital and walked to La Perla just a few blocks away. On entering he saw Alan sitting at a window table. The owner Chef was speaking to him and pushing specials for dinner.

"Hi Alan. Casey is doing much better, but she will have at least six weeks of rehab. Right now she is trussed up to a contraption that keeps her arm elevated. It does not look comfortable. Still a lot better to see her like this than the alternative in a box."

"Agreed, the office called while you were at the hospital. The young Lady has been identified as Helen Matsumoto from San Francisco. One problem down. Now, who is pulling the strings?"

" I think we both know who that is. Christian Allyson is most likely. He would be trying to protect his cash cow."

"I agree Duncan, but that makes the two of us as possible targets on going. He must know we are aware of him and that would be bad news. "

"There is a limit to what he can do. I am going to run up to New Jersey and see what I can get out of one of the three men that work for ALLTEL."

"I assume you are going to fly to Newark and rent a car to get to Ridgewood."

"Yes, leaving tomorrow morning on one of the commuter jets. I won't have time to stop in on Casey."

"Don't worry. I will swing by, and make sure she has everything she needs. I might try and get the President to make a patient visit as well. It can't hurt to have the Hospital staff see you have friends in high places."

"Thanks Alan, and thank the President. Now let's get something to eat. What did the Chef say is good tonight?"

"He is pushing the Dover Sole Almondine."

"Sounds good to me. How about a bottle of wine?"

"Done, now to catch the waiter's eye." The waiter did see they were ready, came over, took the order and left. Their dinner arrived and a friend of Alan's also appeared.

"Hi Alan. Nice to see you again."

"Ann, this is Duncan Innes, an investigator with us. Ann is an FDA expert that happens to live in the Restaurants building. I have known her for many years."

"Good evening Duncan, a pleasure to meet you. I hope you enjoy dinner. Good bye Alan it's back to work."

"Good bye Ann, nice to see you again."

Duncan nodded and Ann left.

"Known her long?"

CHAPTER 28

NEW JERSEY

"Yes, years ago she was an investigator for the FDA and was called to the Hill to testify on a drug issue. I was also there for another reason. We got to speaking and I enjoyed the conversation. We have been friends ever since. I have dinner or lunch with her from time to time. She is a good contact and very well-connected in the Senate and the House. Since everything in the town is about who you know, she is a contact worth keeping."

'Understood. Do you want coffee?"

"No thanks. I can drop you off at your Condo if you wish on my way home?"

"Thanks, saves me an Uber trip. Thanks for dinner and any help you can offer Casey. It is appreciated."

"Duncan, do you think the president will act on what we told him?"

"No, he will wait and see what I can find out. No point in rocking the boat until he knows the risks."

"Let's wait and see what I get in New Jersey and go from there."

They both left La Perla and headed to Alan's car. The ride was short to Duncan's Condo. They talked about the meeting with the president but agreed, nothing to be done for the time being. Duncan got out at his home and headed inside as Alan drove away to his house in the suburbs. Once in the condo, Duncan dialed Marlee. Time to check-in.

"Sorry, I know it is late. But I wanted to hear your voice."

"It's OK Duncan. I am glad to hear from you. I have to get up early for work, so this is a good wake up call."

"We did play telephone tag yesterday. I thought you were there still in Stellenbosch."

"I was, I came back late afternoon. Had a nice time and my friends all want to meet you. What they really want is an audition. They are all very protective."

'Good, and certainly, I can make a dress rehearsal when I am next in Cape Town."

"Any idea when that will be? I miss you."

' I should know latest next week when I can get away. I've had a bit of a bother here today."

"What happened?"

"An old friend of mine was shot in the line of duty. She is a policewoman. So far she is looking okay, but a bit worn from wear. I am sure she will recover."

"Were you involved?"

"Only indirectly, I was nearby when she was hit and could help her get to the hospital. "

"Well that's good. How good an old friend?"

" I have known her for over ten years and followed her career with interest. She has helped me out in my job on a few occasions, so I remain interested in her activities." For Duncan, this was all true and additional information did not need to be supplied.

"Well that sounds benign."

"It is, and I am going to New Jersey in the morning on another project. Right now, I need a few hours of sleep. I can call you again at a more reasonable time tomorrow afternoon here around 10 pm your time."

"That works, I have a slow day tomorrow. Sweet dreams, I am thinking of you."

"And I you. Until tomorrow, have a good day."

Duncan reluctantly hung up and began to put together what he would need in New Jersey. A quick call to the Marriott Hotel in Saddle Brook, N.J. confirmed a reservation for two nights. His Hertz pick-up had been confirmed and flight booking so nothing more to do there. A simple carry-on would do it for the trip. A shower and off to bed for at least four hours of sleep. He realized how lucky he had been to have Casey with him earlier. Not so lucky for her or Helen Matsumoto. The morning came very quickly. Out of bed, a cup of coffee, and an Uber call to get to National. One hour later he was at the gate for his flight to Newark. The airport was packed as usual and his plane was no exception.

Coffee and a Danish would have to do for breakfast. The line at Cinnabon was long and slow. Most of the people looked like salespeople going out on the road. Airport shrill announcements were constantly blaring on the intercom system. Travel was no longer a fun or an exciting experience. None of the other passengers that he could see appeared happy to be flying. Still, it beat driving or walking for that matter. He boarded when his row was called, along with five others in the next rows. Still had to duck through the entranceway of the plane. The obligatory smiles of the stewardesses greeted him as he moved down the center aisle and headed for his row. He always took an aisle seat. There was more room for his long legs. He had to be careful when the carts came through or be hit in a knee. The flight itself was short. He went, on landing straight to Hertz with his carry- on bag. The reservation board had his name up and spot 18 as his. Fifteen minutes later he was out of the lot and heading towards the thruway for Saddle Brook. The throughway was packed with trucks. New York had an insatiable appetite for goods and food. New Jersey was the loading point for everything that went into the city. The Turnpike, Route Three, Route Four and Seventeen, 46 all spilled out in Manhattan, making for a large parking lot when over-taxed. The tunnels would be crowded whether the Lincoln or Holland. Regardless of the fans, the fumes would be heavy for the drivers. Duncan stayed on the Turnpike and only switched over onto the Interstate to Saddle Brook before the George Washington Bridge feeder. Traffic was lighter here, so he arrived at the hotel at midday. The room was a typical Marriott with the same pictures on the wall as all other Marriotts around the world. Someone had once explained that this was deliberate to give you a sense of familiarity as if coming home. The hotel Restaurant was plain and simple. The choices mirrored every hotel restaurant in the country. Hamburger, Club Sandwich some non-descript chicken and salads on offer. He opted for the club sandwich and called Casey while he waited.

"How are you feeling?"

"Still sore , but ok. Alan came by and believe it or not the President dropped in. He caused quite a commotion. The staff has certainly become friendlier and more solicitous since he was here. He did say he had met you and sends his regards."

'Thanks, but I am sure that was Alan's doing."

'Yes, he brought some lovely flowers and apologized for sending you out of town. Do you know when you will be back?"

"No, I have only just arrived and having lunch, then off to Ridgewood."

"What is in Ridgewood?"

"Another Banker being vetted for the Federal Reserve. I am just doing some due diligence."

"Well, Duncan, you do know that Ridgewood is the home of the original Yuppieviille?"

"So it would seem. In any case, it shouldn't take more than two days and then I will be back and visit you."

" Great, hopefully, I will be out of this harnesss when you are back."

'Don't rush it, Casey. Do what the doctors say and pay attention to the PT people. Take it easy now, there will be enough for you to do later."

'Sorry we put you through all of this. I was the lady's target and but for you I could be in that bed or worse."

"At least it is over and it was a righteous shooting. Be careful though, there may be some others with similar intent out there."

'Will do, but for now I am off to Yuppieville per your description. Have a good day and order food I through your friends or call Alan. He can get you some real food delivered. Maybe some donuts, muffins, etc. for your nursing staff taking care of you."

"Good idea, I will call him if you think that it's okay?"

"He will love to help. Besides, he thinks you are cute and wants to be on your side." Duncan laughed, said his goodbyes, and headed for the car park. The first pass in Ridgewood would be by the offices of ALLTEL. A basic reconnaissance mission. Things were starting to look like they were coming to a close. It would be up to the president whether he wanted to do something with the V.P., which probably depended on what Alan wanted to do with him.

CHAPTER 29

ALLTEL

The ALLTEL office was in a once-private house off of Chestnut Street behind the Ridgewood YMCA. He drove past not really expecting to see much of anything. Three cars in the front of the house on a long drive-way, otherwise no activity. Two of the cars were very dusty. The third had been recently washed. Nothing could be seen through the front picture window. Continuing on Chestnut and then finally turning round and heading back to Franklin Street. A cup of coffee sounded like a good idea now. He would return around five pm and see who came out of the building. It had been a long time since he was last on a stakeout, but he needed to know how many people were there and what they looked like. Further up on Chestnut was the Cookshop Eatery and Bakery. That would be ideal to kill an hour or so. Time for a call to Marlee via What's App. That would be the cheapest call.

"Hello, Marlee?"

'Yes, is that you Duncan?"

'Yes, it is. How was your day?"

"As good as can be expected. We had a delegation of

Kuwaitis here today. Assisi was among them, but said very little."

"What did they want?" he was nervous as he asked. This could compromise her position in the Bank.

"With the death of Gert, they wanted to know who the lead on their account would be going forward. Fortunately, the Chairman, Peter Haag, jumped in and said he would personally take care of all of their needs. If there were any issues or special requests they should be addressed to him."

The Delegation seemed satisfied with that arrangement. Their first order of business was another major transfer of 20 million dollars. Same routing but without Levick as the addressee. They had come up with another name in London at the London Exchange. That will go out tomorrow through my department."

"Ok Marlee, let's stay low-key on this. I do not want you compromised at all. Thanks for the heads up. Watch out for Assisi, he is a bad guy."

"Will do, but right now Peter has positioned me to look absolutely harmless to them. It should stay that way."

"Get a good night's sleep. I still think of you every day."

"How is your friend, the one that was shot?"

"She is recovering well. All excited about a big promotion she just received. I think it will be hard for the hospital to keep her inside. She was never one to relax and take it easy."

"I will try and call again tomorrow, but can't promise. I am traveling right now and only be home tomorrow or the next day. I will call though. If you need me or need anything text me and I will call as soon as possible." They said their good byes yet again. Coffee had arrived with a muffin at the Cook-shop. There were a few patrons enjoying late lunches or just coffee at other tables. All patrons seemed like locals except for Duncan. The waitress was efficient and ensured his cup was full of hot coffee. He killed a little less than an hour at the table.

"I am glad your friend is recovering well. Happier still when you tell me when you are coming back to Cape Town."

Duncan paid the check and went back out to his car. He decided to park in the back lot of the YMCA. From there he could see ALLTEL's front porch. There still remained three cars in the driveway. They were too far away to get license plates number. Fifteen minutes later his patience in waiting paid off. A large black SUV with government plates pulled up to the house. The driver jumped out und opened the rear door. Christian Allyson stepped out and headed into the house. He carried a small briefcase. The house door opened and in he walked. The driver returned to the front and got back into the SUV. There was really nothing else for Duncan to do at this point. He decided to remain as invisible as possible and see what happened. Two people came out of the house a few minutes later and got into the waiting cars. They drove off leaving one car behind. Ten minutes later the SUV returned. The driver again jumped out and held the door open for the now-returning Christian Allyson. The SUV pulled away and headed back towards the town center. Another man came out the door just behind Christian. He approached the third car and got in. This time, Duncan let the car pull forward and then followed at a safe distance. The car turned on Franklin and started toward the next town Glen Rock. Duncan kept his distance but followed as the driver turned towards Route 208. Both headed towards New York City on 208. Traffic was again light making it easy to follow without being obvious. The driver pulled into a Holiday Inn just off Route 208 on Route Seventeen. Duncan drove past two blocks, and circled around in time to see the driver come out of reception and head back to his car for a case. Duncan pulled into an empty slot three cars down. With his side mirror, Duncan could watch the man return to the hotel. It no longer mattered if he was seen as he planned to take the driver in his room. You can't keep trying to have someone killed and not expect push back.

The man was just starting to climb the stairs to an upper floor when Duncan came in. He immediately followed and was not challenged by the front desk person. If you looked like you belonged, you did. As he came around the corner in the stairwell, the door to the hallway was closing. Duncan hurried up and caught it before it banged closed. The driver was at the first room to the right fumbling with his key. Duncan came through the door just behind him. He shoved the man onto the bed. No resistance, just a gasp of surprise.

"What do you want?" the man said.

" Who are you?" Duncan said this with the authority of a very big man.

"Sean Riley, why? Is this a robbery?

"No, but I do have some questions as a Police officer." Duncan flashed his credpack which no one ever looked at in any case.

"Do you have a warrant to be in here?"

"Do not need one. You fall under the Terrorist Act. Let's see some I.D.."

CHAPTER 30

RIDGEWOOD

He handed over his wallet with driver's license and a business card saying he was Sean Riley, CFO Accountant for ALLTEL an NGO in Ridgewood New Jersey. A few credit cards and small receipts rounded out the contents.

"Well Mr. Riley, we have reason to believe that you are fronting for a terrorist group out of the Middle East."

"That is absurd. We supply telecommunications to third-world countries. More importantly, our CEO is Christian Allyson, the Vice President of the United States son."

"Interesting and what exactly do you do?"

" I keep the books, payroll, account receivables, and payables for ALLTEL."

"Does that include washing money from other countries Mr. Riley" Riley blanched at the reference to washing money.

"We do no such thing and what is your name again?" He was starting to get belligerent.

"My name is Innes. You have an opportunity here to explain what ALLTEL does and how money comes in and out or we can go straight to jail, your call." The hook was set, now it was up to Riley to try and wriggle free.

'This is all nonsense. Arrest me if you want to otherwise, get out of my room." The fear was wearing off of Mr. Riley. It would return later when Riley realized nothing had happened but would in the future. he needed to get to a phone away from this man Innes.

'Mr. Riley, do not leave town or take any trips until I have cleared you. Do you understand?"

"I do. I will be at work for the rest of the week."

"Good, think it over. Is it worth protecting someone that might send you to jail for a very long time? Have a good night."

Duncan left and returned to his car. One call to do, Alan and bring him up to date.

"Hi Duncan. What have you found out?"

"Well, Alan, I saw the V.P.'s son go into ALLTEL's office this afternoon. I also accosted Sean Riley who is the accountant or CFO of ALLTEL. I think I put the fear of God into him."

"And why?"

" I think he will immediately report my visit, which should shake something out of the trees."

"As long as what falls is not another assassin. Doesn't matter, we need this investigation to come to a close. I think my tweaking them today will get a major reaction. We should be ready. Beef up your security in case they choose you first. I think Christian probably has headed home, so I do not expect to see him again today. The other two I am not sure of at this point. Christian was in a government car. Perhaps Secret Service people driving. Did you ever find out anything about Hans Ritter or Erich Kochan?"

" I only know rumor. Ritter is an ex-special forces type, very dangerous. Kochan was a member of the German Mountain Alpine Forces. Also dangerous. Be careful around those two.'

"Will do, I am coming back to D.C,. tonight. I'll call if anything happens."

"Have a good flight. As a side note, Casey is doing very well. She is getting a lot of first-class attention after the President's visit. I also ensured a decent meal and treats for the staff both day and night.'

"Thanks Alan. I owe you one."

"No debt due, just be careful. It was my pleasure to help Casey."

Duncan's plane landed at National at 8;30 pm. He caught an Uber to his condo. Things were starting to look up. Now he was on the offensive rather than just reacting to others..

Duncan's Condo was as he left it. He took a shower made a sandwich and called Marlee. She was not answering. Casey on the other hand was still bedridden.

"How are you feeling?"

"Fine Duncan. Still a little sore, but they keep me stocked with their laLa juice so I do not feel much pain. I do however, sleep well and often."

"That's good. Sleep will let you heal faster. How are the staff treating you?"

Since the President's visit and the donuts and muffins, you would think I am Queen of the May. I really can't thank Alan enough for the gesture. I owe him one now."

"Don't worry about it, he doesn't expect anything."

Duncan could hear the room's television in the back ground. A loud breaking News announcement just came on as he listened..

CHAPTER 31

A V.P. DISTRAUGHT

"What is the news Casey?"

"The V.P.'s son has been shot and killed. "

"What?" Duncan told her he would call back but he needed to speak with Alan.

"I thought you might call. Christian was gunned down near his Condo. He is dead. One Secret Service man is also injured, but expected to live. It just happened about one hour ago. The agent killed the assailant who shot both Christian and himself. So far not identified. I know you wanted to shake the trees, but this is a little extreme."

"Agreed. I assume that Riley called my visit in and someone decided we were too close. Removing Christian essentially removes the trail. Can you get the NSA to look into phone calls to Kuwait or London in the past three hours. I suspect there will be calls to both. One probably to Assisi as he seems to be the center point. I am sorry for the V.P.'s loss, but they were playing a bit fast and loose."

"I will look into this Duncan but be careful. I want to know who the assassin was. I should have his name and I.D. shortly. I will call you back. "

"Thanks Alan. I am at home if you find anything." Duncan hung up. A few minutes later Alan called back.

"Hi Duncan, The shooter of the V.P.'s son was a Erich Kochan. Seems rather odd that he would take such a risk with Secret Service Agents about. Granted, Christian only had two men assigned, but they are all very good at their jobs. The White House is now directly involved. A press conference on all of this will start in about twenty five minutes. CNN will carry it so you can be updated by that. The V.P. has declined to speak with the Press. Let's meet in my office tomorrow morning at 9:30. We can go over what we are prepared to tell the President at that time. I know he will be calling shortly wanting an update on what we found since our last meeting."

"Okay, see you in the morning. Right now, I am turning the T.V. on".

Duncan was greeted by, This is CNN with breaking news. The Vice President's son has been shot outside of his home in the Foggy Bottom area. So far, no motive has been found. One Secret Service Agent also took a bullet and he shot the assassin. The shooter was an Erich Kochan, who worked at ALLTEL an NGO run by Christian Allyson. The Washington Police Chief will hold a press Conference in the morning at 9 am with more details. Vice President Allyson has been reluctant to speak with the press and asks we respect this tragic event for his family via his Press Secretary. CNN will break into any ongoing programs if new information becomes available. Right now, we are returning to our scheduled programs.

Duncan called Casey back.

"Quite a busy hour." Christian Allyson has been shot, I am sure you are aware. All channels will be carrying that."

"Anything to do with you Duncan?"

"No, why would you ask?"

"I know you were suspicious of the V.P. for calling you and Alan into his office and thought you might know something. It is really rather sad when one of your children is killed."

"I agree, but not anything to do with me. Besides, right now, I want you to worry about yourself, get well and feel better."

"I feel remarkedly good right now. The Juice is holding off the pain and I am getting more sleep and rest than I have had in years. Not the recommended way to take time off."

"Got it. Take the time. You will need it. Get a good night's sleep." Duncan thought he better call Alan back. Someone needed to pick Sean Riley up. Riley was the weakest link in the entire ALLTEL operation. If they were willing to kill the V.P.'s son, Riley would become a simple calculation. Running the books, he would just know too much. Alan agreed and said he would get someone from the FBI to pick him up in New Jersey. They would bring him back to D.C. and spend some time debriefing Riley on what he knew.

" Add another issue, Alan. Remember the third man, Hans Ritter. He is still out there. If Erich Kohan was the shooter of Christian, where is Hans Ritter? Picking up Riley will be easy. That will not be the case with Ritter."

I will see if I can get the FBI to put out an APB on Ritter with an 'approach with caution advisory'. Last we knew he was still in Ridgewood, but we also thought Kochan was there. If he has left Ridgewood, he could be anywhere. Stay safe Duncan. These people seem to be tying off loose ends, which means you. Ritter and Kochan were equally dangerous. He is the threat right now!"

"See you in the morning. Have a good night."

Both men hung up and retired for the night. Duncan was exhausted from the trip and what was left over from the Casey shooting. The morning would come quick enough and did.

CNN, FOX News all carried a repeat of the news conference, plus remarks from the President. The V.P. was going to take some family time off to grieve and prepare for the funeral. The President expressed condolences. A short bio of Erich Kochan was made available to various news outlets. It did describe his military days and work for the NGO ALLTEL. No motive had been assigned to the shooter. There was the possibility that Kochan was about to be terminated by ALLTEL for poor performance, this was from the Vice President's office. No further announcements were expected. The D.C. police claimed they were working closely with the FBI to ensure there was no terrorist connection to the shooting. As for now, it looked like a disgruntled employee had gone off the rails. Duncan did his morning exercises and prepared to leave for Alan's office. A short call to Casey to just say hello and wish her a good day followed.

The Uber driver, one of the thousands of African students, was very quiet. They pulled up in front of Alan's office block to several police cars. Duncan left a tip and a five-star rating on his cell phone. A few minutes later and he was in Alan's office.

"Why all the police out there?"

"My FBI friends thought a show of force might be a good idea. They had picked up Riley and started to sweat him. Your name and mine came up as persons of interest to ALLTEL. With Christian's murder and the tie to ALLTEL, they thought it wise to set up some protection for all. I doubt we are targets anymore. Too much has already come out for us to be a threat."

'There is always the revenge issue."

'No, Duncan, that would lead to more exposure for someone. We need to have Ritter found, as the last real threat and as a side note, I would like to know where Assisi is right now. As I said last night, the President does want to see us this morning at 11 am. We can ride over there together. How much do we want to tell him and what about your tweaking of Riley. We both think that is what got Christian killed. We were too close. Now with Riley in custody maybe that will do it. Revenge is however a good motivator. With Christian dead, the Kuwaiti's and Gulf States no longer have their conduit into the government. Their influence via the Super Pacs will also be diminished. The money people behind Assisi can't be happy right now. This entire operation took a long time to establish and will not be easy to replace. The Gulf States have to be concerned with what is going on with the Iranians. Hamas going crazy in Israel remains a distraction. Iran's navy buildup is quietly progressing. They can close the gulf whenever they want and there is nothing we can do about it."

"There is nothing we can do about that. The best we can do is close off the entire Kuwait access, assuming it is the Kuwaitis?"

"I do not think there is any doubt left. There is most defi-nitely a tie from Assisi to Christian and beyond. That is effec-tively now over, but the Kuwaitis will not want anyone to know of their involvement. What is important is to remove the visible ties to Christian. This could easily become an International incident that no one wants."

They both went through the same drill at the White House entrance. I.D.Badges, and escorted to the oval office.

"Gentlemen, thank you again for coming. Please update me on what you know."

Duncan launched into a recap of the Shia Crescent of Power, Assisi from Kuwait and the ties to Christian Allyson via ALLTEL. Proof of involvement by the Vice President was not evident. It would however be hard to believe that he did not know what his son was up to at this time. Duncan recounted the conversations with Riley and the subsequent murder of Christian Allyson shortly thereafter. The coincidence was just too much to believe random. All this was followed with Christian being shot by Erich Kochan of ALLTEL. He did describe Hans Ritter as a player with Kochan. They were now actively looking for Ritter. The FBI was also looking as well.

"Well, let me handle the Vice Presidents side of all this. I suspect he will suddenly wish to retire to mourn his son and withdraw from public service, understandable. This, of course, I will allow. The country can not afford another scandal like Trump or Biden and his son."

What the President would do about Kuwait and the Gulf states would remain to be seen. They were both thanked for their work up to this time. Leaving the Oval Office was a relief for both. Now, only what happened to Ritter made a priority. Once in the car, Alan asked "What do you think?"

"I think his solution of letting the V.P. retire is his only choice. If a trial was pursued against the now dead sons interest or ALLTEL, the hue and cry would be very loud. The V.P. would have to stand trial and have his dirty laundry washed in public. This way the entire issue dies. The president will most likely track the funds to the Super Pacs and use whatever he learns for future leverage. No good disaster should be allowed to vanish without some benefit. That is politics today. There might even be something useful for leverage with Congress on Iran and Israeli issues. So I expect this will all just die quietly without anyone being the wiser."

Two days later the V.P. announced on CNN that he was retiring. Too much grief at the loss of his son. ALLTEL would be shut down and assets turned over to the countries that had accepted the phone services. The President commiserated and wished his V.P. well in the future. One week later, Duncan was back at the deli off Dupont Circle. It was a pity that Casey was not there, but she was still in rehab. When he finished his coffee and bagel, Duncan went back to his condo. Things had been very quiet. Marlee was doing well in her new job and asking when he would return. Casey was coming home to her flat without the arm brace but with what looked like a harness. He sent an email to Marlee that evening saying he would be back for a visit in one week. A vacation was approved by Alan and deserved. She responded with a large smile emoji.

'Hi Duncan. Sorry to call so late, but we think we may know where Ritter is. His profile was flagged yesterday at Dulles. He was boarding a flight to Frankfurt. Since he still holds a German passport no one thought to look closely. A friend at the U.S.Embasssy is going to see if he can find out anything about where Ritter is going or staying. I expect you'll be leaving tomorrow for Frankfurt?"

'Yes I will. Ritter is a loose end. I will check with Otto and see if he can find out anything. I am sure he has friends at immigration. Call me Alan if you hear of Ritters whereabouts. I am going to book my flights now."

"For safety's sake, I am going to appraise the President of your travel plans. Keep me informed."

"You too please, any information on Ritter's go to ground place would be helpful Alan"

"Absolutely. I'll pull every favor I can use to get Ritter's whereabouts. By the way, Riley has struck a plea deal. He has coughed up all the information on the Super PACs, the amounts and to whom they supported. He also threw Christian under the bus with amounts he had taken for himself. The President is very pleased. More leverage. Riley will get no jail time in exchange for his testimony on his complicities in money laundering. The D.A. will not prosecute here, way too political. It is over. The only open issue is Ritter. What does he know and can he hurt the President?"

'We're going to find out, I am off to Frankfurt, tell the President.".

The phone rang for a few minutes or so it seemed.

"Guten Abend"

"Hi Otto, Duncan here, sorry to wake you up, but I am coming to Frankfurt tomorrow. Should be there late in the day."

"This is an unexpected pleasure. Why so sudden?"

"I'll bring you up to date when I get there. Right now I am trying to find a German named Hans Ritter. He probably just arrived in Frankfurt. Any friends in Immigration?"

"Yes, I will run a check and let you know when you arrive. Meet at the Opern Café again as last time?'

"Yes, but make it dinner, say around 20:00, if that works for you?"

"That works, see you tomorrow. Let me get on the phone now and see what I can find out. Have a safe flight and get some sleep on the plane. If it were me, I would take an Ambien just before takeoff and sleep the trip away. See you tomorrow."

They both hung up and Duncan packed a small overnight valise. Dopp kit, change of clothes for two days. Pass port, drivers license, credit cards, and business cards rounded up the needs. If he needed more clothes he could buy them.

Twelve hours later Duncan was in Frankfurt City Center. The Hauptwache was the U-Bahn station. Just a short walk over to the Open Café on the Eschenheimer Landstrassse.

"Hi Duncan, I thought you might come this way. Let's walk together to the Café. The evening crowd had started to thin as they walked past several Restaurants, small coffee shops and bakeries and Jewelers.

"Why are you interested in Hans Ritter? "

"Ritter is involved in ALLTEL, a Company I have been looking into. The long story is involved and contains elements of the Kuwaitis and Assisi." Duncan explained the events to date along with the Ritter connection. It took the entire walk of 15 minutes to go through everything with Otto.

"It sounds dangerous at this point. Your friend being shot, the attempts on your life, and Alans. What's the plan if and when you find Ritter?"

" I want to squeeze him a bit for information on the Middle East connection."

"Why Duncan, do you think he will know anything?"

'He may not, but at least he will know we are aware of him and can find him when we wish."

"But, according to you, the last time you accosted an employee of ALLTEL, the son of the V.P. was killed. What will this meeting mean for the future?"

"It depends on who is paying him. Is he direct with ALLTEL, which is now drying up or is he an agent of the Kuwaiti faction?"

"The good news is I do know where Hans Ritter is headed. He lives in Friedberg. A small city near Bad Homburg. Friedberg's only claim to fame is it was the home of Elvis Pressley in the late 50's and early 60s. The army base was his home. Other than that an agricultural town producing mainly apples. You can catch a train directly there from the Main Station. Here is the address on the Frankfurter Land Strasse."

'Thank you, Otto. How hard was it to find this out?'

'Actually Duncan,, pretty simple. The Government keeps track of people they have trained such as Hans Ritter. When they turn up at a border crossing a note is made. It is just a question of having someone access the database for any available information. As you know in Germany, everybody is required to register their home and where they live. This includes hotels. If a guest arrives they have to give their passports to the front desk. The desk copies this and every evening the police drop by and collect that data. That data is entered into the main Database. It makes it far easier to track criminals or people of interest so to speak."

Otto handed a piece of paper to Duncan just as they arrived at the Opern Café. Duncan glanced at it, put it away in his jacket pocket, and held the door for Otto. They enjoyed dinner together, talked a little bit about Marlee in Cape Town life in Germany in general. Otto waxed euphoric about Marlee's looks, which Duncan seconded. Duncan also said she is not only beautiful but bright and an asset for the South African Bank. A short while later they parted company and Duncan headed back to his old haunt in Bad Homburg. The Park Hotel was both reasonable and comfortable. Better than the big box-type hotels. What the Park lacked in modernity was made up for by friendly efficient staff and a wonderful breakfast buffet.

The morning brought another chance for taking a ride to Friedberg and seeing if he could track down Hans Ritter. Thirty minutes later and Duncan was near the address Otto had supplied. What was concerning were all of the police around Ritter's building. The five-story house looked imposing compared to the others in the neighborhood. He got out of the cab and walked near the police cordon. A few obvious neigh-bors were standing around watching the activity. The blue lights were still flashing when he came up to a man and woman outside of a nearby house. Duncan asked the two, "can either of you speak English?"

Th woman responded yes.

"What happened here?" he asked.

"One of the tenants here had died from what looks like cement poisoning." She laughed as she said it.

'How is that?"

"His body was found this morning on the side of the house. He apparently fell from the top floor and hit the driveway head-first. At least that is what I heard one of the Officers say. I prob-ably have said too much already."

"Quite all right. Anyone know who this was?"

"I heard the name Ritter, but that is all."

"Thank you, I guess I will be on my way. I have a meeting at the Bank this morning."

No point in asking anything further. The police would not talk to him in any case and it would be too complicated to tell them why he cared. He carried on towards a nearby Bank in case the couple got curious. With Ritter dead the only explanation was Assisi was cleaning up any blow back that could arise. Going after Assisi would be fruitless. He would be long gone if he was involved in Ritter's death and carried Diplomatic immunity. The only course of action left was to call Alan, bring him up to date. The last lead that might have supported evidence for the President was now dead. He called Otto first and explained what he found."

"Did you kill him?"

"No Otto, I found the scene filled with cops, so I left. A neighbor filled me in on what had happened. I am heading back to the hotel, will book my flight to Cape Town as there is nothing more to do here."

"Well Duncan, have a good trip. As always, when in Frankfurt please call me. Also, my best to Marlee. She always will have a friend here and she should know that."

"Thanks, Otto, I will tell her. Thanks again for all of your help in this business. The Federal Reserve is very grateful for your aid and if there is anything we can do for you, let me or Alan know. I suspect the President will also be thankful for your efforts. Now I have to give Alan a call and let him know what has happened. Too many bodies on this investigation, but thankfully I think it is over. We will keep an eye on Assisi, now that we know he pulls the strings. Alan can handle that, I am on vacation."

"Have a good flight to South Africa. Goodbye Duncan, always a pleasure."

'Thanks, Otto, goodbye."

Now it was a waiting game for the other shoe to drop. Assisi was in the wind, Germany couldn't find him and more than likely he was back home in Kuwait.

The next evening found Duncan at the door to Disa Park in Cape Town. He rang Marlee's Condo on the Resident's panel. She answered with, "Yes" over the intercom.

"Honey I am home!"

He was thrilled to be back and to see Marlee again, but the question would always be for how long?